D1496178

THE BREAKER
WHISTLE BLOWS

*Mining Disasters and Labor Leaders
in the Anthracite Region*

by

Ellis W. Roberts

Anthracite Press
Scranton, Pennsylvania
1984

Library of Congress Cataloging in Publication Data

Roberts, Ellis W. 1911–
The Breaker Whistle Blows

1 United States—Economic Conditions—To 1960

2 United States—Labor—History

3 United States—Politics—History

4 Coal Mining—United States
   History I Title

ISBN   0917445-00-5

© Scranton Anthracite Museum Associates

To the memory of immigrant
anthracite coal mine workers
and their families

The Pennsylvania Historical and Museum Commission is the commonwealth agency responsible for preserving and interpreting the history and culture of Pennsylvania. It oversees a state-wide network of historical sites and museums, an archival and record management program, a preservation and historical register program, and an historical division with responsibility for topical studies and research. The Commission also assists and works with other historical agencies and institutions, as well as governmental bodies, to preserve the Commonwealth's heritage.

The Scranton Anthracite Museum is part of the Commission's Anthracite Museum Complex. The Complex includes the Ashland Anthracite Museum, which emphasizes the technology of mining and processing anthracite; Eckley Miners Village, an original mid-nineteenth century mining town, which relates the everyday life of the miner and his family; and the Scranton Anthracite Museum, which interprets the broad topics of immigration and ethnicity, transportation, labor organization and management practices, the growth of industry, and the rise of towns and cities.

The Scranton Anthracite Museum Associates is an organization formed to assist with programming and development of the Scranton Anthracite Museum. It sponsors lectures and film series, tours, exhibits, research and publications, and general Museum development. It is the local, public arm of the Museum, which directly ties the Museum to its local heritage and community support.

Anthracite Press
Anthracite Museum of Scranton
Bald Mountain Road R.D.#1
Scranton, PA. 18504

Acknowledgments

I am indebted to a number of persons who have helped me with the research and writing of this volume.

Miss Joan Costello, head librarian of the Osterhout Free Library in Wilkes-Barre, and many of her staff have been most gracious in providing books and newspapers. Miss Jeanette Viglotti, head of the circulation department, and Miss Ruth Richards, head of the reference department, were especially helpful, as were reference librarians Elaine Homick, Diane Suffren and Bernadette McGough.

My wife, Mary Sullivan Roberts, proof-read all of the material several times. Her editorial patience often turned chaos into cohesiveness.

Special gratitude goes to those who directed me to valuable resource material: The Reverend James J. Doyle, C. S. C., Chairman of the Theology Department of King's College in Wilkes-Barre; Monsignor Donald A. McAndrews, Executive Director of Social Services of the Scranton Diocese; the late Attorney Fred Gendral, perhaps the only coal miner to obtain degrees from Harvard University and Harvard Law School; and James Reinmiller, Director of the Hazleton Public Library.

My most profound gratitude goes to Dr. David Salay, Director of the Pennsylvania Anthracite Museum Complex, to Mary Ann Landis, Curator of the Eckley Miners' Village, and to Hugh Oliver, most knowledgeable in the technologies of printing and publishing.

Dr. Jule Ayers, my friend and pastor, a present-day counterpart of Father Curran of an earlier period, helped me to sustain an interest in working men and women. His dedication to the rights and obligations of those who work with hand and brain has made him a community pastor to both labor and management.

Dr. William H. Seiner, while director of the Wyoming Historical and Geological Society, helped to support my belief in the need for a single volume of these anthracite highlights. Rev. William Lewis, director of the Lackwanna Historical Society, was a key person in directing me to Scranton sources. Gilbert Schappert was one of the first to read the manuscript and respond with many helpful notations.

v

Gary Yenkowski gave me specific suggestions after his enthusiastic and detailed analysis of the manuscript. The readings by David Wazeter and James Gittens stimulated my efforts as did the inquisitive interest of Steven and Scott Shemo.

My brother, Thomas Roberts, who suffered a severe injury in mining, has contributed immeasurably to this volume. His insights and reflections were vividly real, and always historically accurate.

I am especially grateful to Patti Moore Munoz, who typed my first draft with skill and care, and to Margaret M. Hannon, most cooperative and expert in her work, for typing several revisions and the complete final draft, and to Cathy Bozar for typing parts of the revisions.

The Knox Disaster has been described here as a mine tragedy and not as a legal case-study; however, I am indebted to former District Attorneys, Albert Aston and Stephen Teller, for insights into the structure and administration of the Knox Coal Company.

A few survivors of the Knox Disaster supplied realistic memories of coal mining at that colliery. Anthony Remus, who quickly walked to safety on the day of the disaster, and Allan Kanarr, not involved in the incidents of that particular day, gave me a great deal of help in understanding the Knox problems. Myron Thomas, assistant foreman of the Knox Colliery, during a lecture at Scranton's Anthracite Museum and later at his home, graciously gave me his time and scrapbook for research.

Judith Tierney, reference librarian of King's College, enabled me to use the papers of John Mitchell, the complete microfilms of the originals which are at Catholic University in Washington, D.C. Mary Alice Moss, granddaughter of John Mitchell, graciously provided material about her grandfather. Nancy Abbott Cohen of the King's College library staff provided information on Terence V. Powderly. Thanks to Georgetta Nelson, the complete account of the Avondale Disaster, as reported in *The Scranton Weekly Republican* in September, 1869, is available in a typed manuscript at the Osterhout Free Library in Wilkes-Barre. Finally, I thank Joseph Kologe for taking time to escort me over the Knox Coal Company property, describing the geography of the exterior shaft openings, and the site of the tragedy.

The illustration of the Eckley Breaker is the photography and special art work of Curtis Salonick. Other art work of the breaker whistle is that of Pam Ross. I am especially grateful to both for their fitting interpretations.

Table of Contents

ix

CHAPTER I

The Breaker Whistle Blows

The breaker whistle, a piercing scream of steam, once re-verberated over the valleys and hills of the anthracite region of northeastern Pennsylvania. The high-pitched shrill of the whistle started and ended the workday at every anthracite colliery. It was a feature of everyday life, familiar to man, woman, and child. The breaker whistle had a more dramatic use and sinister meaning as well. At any time of the day or night, the penetrating whistle was the telegrapher of tragedy and a call for help. Whenever an explosion, a fall of rock, a threat of gas, or a flood halted the production of coal, the breaker whistle sent a paralyzing shiver of fear through the mining community. In times of discord, during the disputes between the miners and the mine owners, the breaker whistle could be the herald of unemployment or the symbol of sol-idarity, when it notified the miners of a strike or lockout. The breaker whistle, wailing in the winter wind or in the calm of summer, was at once the town crier and the liberty bell of every anthracite coal patch, borough, or city.

Between 1830 and 1859, more than nine billion tons of anthracite coal were mined by Welsh, English, Irish, Scotch, German, Italian, and Slavic mine workers. These new Amer-icans, in a strip of land only twenty-five miles long and thirty-five miles wide in northeastern Pennsylvania, produced ninety-nine per cent of all the anthracite coal mined in the United States.

The wealth produced by anthracite mining was greater than the total value of the mined gold, silver, lead, and aluminum. It was more than three times the value of copper and two and one half times more than that of iron ore.

The Breaker Whistle Blows describes selected events and personalities of this era. The work has been organized around two interesting observations: each of the three major mining disasters—Avondale, Twin Shaft, and Baltimore Tunnel—sheds light on the ethnic migration to the anthracite region and the ethnic composition of the mine labor force; each of the major mining disasters has been followed by the emergence of a major labor champion.

The victims of the first of these tragedies, the Avondale Disaster, were predominantly Welsh men and boys. Many of them were recent mining recruits from Wales. The labor leader emerging after Avondale was Terence V. Powderly, a president of the Knights of Labor. The Pittston Twin Shaft cave-in suffocated fifty-eight men who were mostly of Irish descent. This tragedy, and that of the Lattimer Massacre, attracted the attention of the young, new United Mine Workers' president, John L. Mitchell. The Baltimore Tunnel explosion, in the East End of Wilkes-Barre, killed ninety-two men, most of whom were of Polish, Slovak, Lithuanian, or Russian descent. This tragedy was followed by the emergence of a labor leader who dominated the American scene for the next half century, John L. Lewis.

From the end of the Civil War until 1960, a period of approximately one hundred years, the United States became the industrial powerhouse of the world. How and why it did lies in the topical histories of coal, steel, rubber, chemicals, textiles, machinery, and oil. Coal mining was a key industry, and no definitive history of the industrial explosion in the United States can ignore the Anthracite Era between the time of the Avondale Disaster in 1869 and the death knell of the anthracite industry, the Knox Mine Disaster of 1959. While the ethnic tragedies and the biographies of the emerging labor leaders described here are but a small part of the anthracite story, they are by no means insignificant to an

2

understanding of the industrial history of the United States. The chapters on land subsidence caused by the mining of anthracite coal, and the final chapter on the Knox Disaster are highlights of anthracite history which surmount ethnic divisions and demand public as well as labor leadership.

As we read of the tragic mine accidents and the emergence of labor leaders, the struggle of miners against their exploitation, and the other problems of the industry, we see a picture of what was once called the anthracite problem. The problem was summarized in this way: Anthracite coal was a valuable national resource concentrated in a tiny geographic area. Millions of consumers depended on it as did thousands of workers. Consumers wanted lower prices. Labor wanted higher wages. Owners wanted greater profits. The coal operators who owned land, mines, and coal-carrying railroads controlled the production and distribution of their products. With monopolistic control over the coal industry, the owner-operators dominated both workers and consumers.

The anthracite industry was a high risk one. Coal was mined at great human costs. In 1907, those killed numbered 918. In 1913, there were 624 mine workers killed out of a work force of 175,310. The mortality rate was twice that of the railroad industry. But the plea of workers and the union for a greater share in the profits was not based solely on the fear of death or accident but also on the desire to survive. The cost of living for a family of six in the anthracite area in 1912 was estimated to be $718.00 per year. If a miner worked every day in 1912, he could earn $800.00. However, a laborer making about $2.50 per day and working his average of 257 days would earn less than $650.00 per year.

As the anthracite industry grew and prospered, the concerns for profits and high dividends kept wages down. Whenever labor was able to obtain increases in pay rates, the consumer and not the company paid the increases. The cost of coal to the consumer inevitably increased after any rise in wages.

The outlook for the anthracite coal industry was analyzed by economists before World War I. Their opinion was that no industry could continue with such an unbalanced and exploitative philosophy. The discrepancies between some of the highest dividends in America and labor costs were unhealthy, to say the least. The anthracite industry also was condemned by both the executive branch of government in Pennsylvania and by the Federal Trade Commission. Pennsylvania's Governor Gifford Pinchot noted in 1923 that despite differences in mining costs, the companies' sales prices of coal were uncannily uniform. The Federal Trade Commission found exorbitant profits among anthracite wholesalers. Both wholesalers and retailers in Boston, New York, and Philadelphia worked on profits from $2.50 to $6.25 a ton. And despite the different margins, the price of coal to the consumer remained constantly high. Such arbitrary price-fixing opened the market for competition by other fuels: coke, bituminous coal, natural gas, and petroleum. The argument that unions or high labor costs were responsible for the decline of the anthracite coal industry does not appear to be valid.

The industry flourished in World War I, nearly collapsed in the Depression, was temporarily rejuvenated in World War II, but expired in the 1950's. In its last days, all too late, the industry adopted some marketing and advertising innovations, but, by that time, gas and oil had replaced coal for home heating and industrial power. Today, in the 1980's, the northern anthracite fields in the Scranton/Wilkes-Barre area are closed. The deep mines are either worked out or flooded. Some sporadic surface mining is evident. The fields in Carbon, Luzerne, Schuylkill, and Northumberland Counties produce a very limited quantity, about 5 million tons, an insignificant tonnage compared to the 99 million tons produced in 1917.

4

In several chapters, notably the first on the Avondale Mine Disaster, the two chapters on Terence Powderly and the Knights of Labor, and again in the chapter on the Lattimer Massacre, the author has used original material rather than his own paraphrasing. The Avondale quotations gave us the flavor of the original reporting of the first major tragedy in anthracite history. The rather lengthy excerpts from *The Path I Trod*, the autobiography of Terence Powderly, are included to give the readers a precise picture of the by-laws of the Knights of Labor, an intriguing organization unlike any other labor body in the history of the American labor movement.

The confrontation between Terence Powderly, as Mayor of Scranton, and the Right Reverend William O'Hara, Bishop of Scranton, is Powderly's version. Acknowledging that it may be self-serving, if not completely biased, it is quoted at length because it reveals the alienation between the church and first organized labor bodies in the United States. This was a problem that was unresolved until the Encyclicals on Labor of Pope Leo XIII changed the official and unofficial Catholic attitudes.

Parts of the court proceedings of the Lattimer Massacre are produced verbatim. Some of the final plea of the prosecution and almost all of that of the defense is included. The records of the case disappeared from the Luzerne County Court House, and are unavailable except as published in one or two books. Therefore, it was deemed useful to have part of the records available in one more current source. In addition, paraphrasing could not possibly reproduce the drama of the trial.

There are pitfalls in the writing of ethnic history. Rowland Tappan Berthoff in his introduction to the volume *British Immigrants in Industrial America* describes the danger. "In embarking on a history of immigrants of a particular nationality, author and reader may well keep a weather eye out for the shoals on which many books have foundered.

5

All too often their writers, ardent partisans seeking to redress some rankling grievance of their chosen people . . . have grossly over-stated their case. Impressed by schoolbook emphasis on discoverers . . . and military heroes, they have frequently filled their books with names of such persons."

The discoverers and military heroes do not appear here. Neither do kings nor prime ministers—only anthracite coal mine workers, their families, their leaders, and their communities.

The Breaker Whistle Blows is an account of selected highlights of the anthracite heritage. This is a rich heritage, the very essence of industrial America's complex history. It includes not only the story of technological chance and economic development—the introduction of steam engines and the tons of coal mined or iron produced—but also that of the immmigrant workers who came to America to improve their lives and lives of their families, present and future. This work is just a small part of the ethnic saga.

CHAPTER II

A Welsh Tragedy

Avondale Fire, 1869

Two years after the Civil War, a new coal breaker built about a mile south of Plymouth, Pennsylvania, at Avondale, promised a boost for the newly emerging post-Civil War anthracite economy. Constructed at a cost of $80,000, a sizable sum in 1867, the new breaker of the Avondale Colliery of the Steuben Coal Company was capable of processing about five hundred tons of coal daily.

The coal breaker was the landmark on the surface of any mine, a tall black structure rising several hundred feet. It housed all the machinery for cleaning and sizing the coal and preparing it for market. At Avondale, the new breaker was built on top of the shaft leading to the underground workings to save the expense of hauling coal from the mine to the breaker.

During the summer of 1869, the breaker had been closed because of a strike, but it was reopened on September 2. Four days later, a fire, probably caused by overheating the ventilating furnace[1] in the mine, broke out at the foot of the shaft. The last man to go down the shaft that morning was the stableboss with a bundle of hay for the mules. Perhaps the dry hay fueled the fire. The fire spread up the shaft and ignited the surface breaker. Within minutes flames shot from the base of the shaft upward more than one hundred feet, burning the superstructure and the breaker. The entrance

---

[1] The ventilating furnace produced the steam to power fans circulating air in the mine.

7

was blocked, trapping those inside the mine. The surface engineer, Alex Weir, seeing the blaze of fire shooting up the shaft, blew the breaker whistle and escaped safely. In moments the whole Avondale Breaker was in flames.

To save the trapped men, the rescue workers decided to pump air into the mine. This decision was to become a controversial one. Some contended that the entrapped men had been sealed off, and could have survived until the original fire was extinguished. The new air, intended to save the lives of the miners, fueled the fire into an inferno which ultimately destroyed everything—cage, breaker and the entire aboveground structure. As the horesdrawn fire equipment rushed to the scene, valley residents gathered by the hundreds, concerned and apprehensive about the fate of the trapped miners. The rescuers were spurred on by the belief that the miners might have sealed themselves off with enough air to survive. The uncertainty paralyzed wives, children, and those at the scene.

A *Scranton World* correspondent, writing for his paper on September 11, 1869, in the flowery phraseology of the period described the scene. "Surrounding the fire on every side were hundreds of men, women and children, the female portion of whom were making the air resound with their frantic cries of distress. No persuasion, entreaty, advice nor consolation served to quiet them. This continued for at least an hour when they became quieter as they saw efforts being made to extinguish the flames, and the rest of the day the outbreaks were less frequent, although it was heart-rending to see individual cases of over-mastering grief, which were exhibited among the cabins of the miners."

In moments telegraph wires along the Lackawanna and Bloomsburg tracks crackled with pleas for help and fire engines. The Kingston contingent with a hand engine, Luzerne, and a crew of men from the railroad were first to respond. The Good Will Company from Wilkes-Barre headed by Stanley Woodward came next.

Rescue squads traveled by railroad from Scranton, twenty miles north. The Nay Aug Steamer, the most modern piece of fire fighting equipment arrived. Other help came from the Shamokin and Shenandoah areas. Coalville, now Ashley, sent a contingent of three hundred miners to volunteer for rescue and clearing operations.

After the fire was extinguished, the shaft was piled high with the rubble of the headframe[2] and the burned breaker. A derrick was built over the top of the shaft to help clear the entrance, and after two days of work, plans were made to re-enter the mine.

The rescue efforts began by lowering a dog into the opening. When the dog survived, the first man descended. An on-site correspondent described the experiences of the first man lowered: "Mr. Virtue reports that about halfway down the shaft he found an obstruction which prevented his further descent. A pump was lodged there, on which rested a stick of timber and other obstructions and although there was an opening large enough to go through, he feared to go down, supposing that if he did, the debris would fall upon him. The brattice[3] around the shaft was not much burned. He reported the air perfectly good and not much heated, but that two men would have to go down as they could work together to good advantage. It was thought best to send down fresh men and, accordingly, Charles Jones of Plymouth and Stephen Evans of Nottingham Shaft volunteered. The two men were provided with a hook and a hatchet, and some other tools, and started down."

The Scranton correspondent then reported the happenings in a periodic description of rescue attempts and the agony of the tragedy: "6:35 p.m. They (the two rescuers) gave signals to stop two or three times and were apparently en-

---

[2] The frame or housing for the wheels and pulleys lowering or raising the cage, the crude elevator carrying men or coal. The headframes first constructed of wood, were later iron or steel.

[3] Planking used to support the walls or roof of a mine.

gaged in clearing away obstructions. 7:02 p.m. Signal to slack off. They were then seen from above to be at the bottom and to get out from the bucket. A season of suspense followed. 7:08 p.m. A smothered sound is heard, as of heavy pounding some distance from the bottom of the shaft, and it was supposed above that it was upon brattice-work being built to close up the gangway by the buried men, and thus prevent the entrance of fire and smoke. 7:12 p.m. Signal to come up. 7:15 p.m. The men emerge from the shaft.

"As soon as Jones and Evans got breath, they reported that they went 70 or 80 yards into a gangway finding three dead mules as they progressed. They finally came to a closed door upon which they pounded, waiting breathlessly for an answering sound from the unfortunate men. But alas! no sound came and they felt compelled to return, having noticed that a cloud of sulphur was pouring out through the crevices in the woodwork of the door. They did not attempt to break down the door, fearing that the sulphur would overpower them in their tracks."

The next two men going down into the mine were Thomas W. Williams and David Jones. Both were suffocated. Their bodies were dragged to the cage and brought to the surface by the next two rescuers, David H. Davis and Benjamin Jones. Further attempts to descend were stopped until a fan could be installed to force air down the shaft.

A meeting was organized in the woods on a nearby hillside where James George, president of a local union, pleaded for a crew of fifty experienced mining men to volunteer as a rescue squad. Men were pouring into the area from throughout northeastern Pennsylvania, and a rescue squad was successfully organized.

After two days of frenzied effort, crews were able to control the poisonous gas, "black damp," or "blue damp" so that rescuers were able to search for the trapped men. Hope still existed that somehow some of them might have been able to seal themselves safely until rescued. Early in the

10

morning on Wednesday, September 8, the hope was dashed. A crew of four men found the bodies of most of the men huddled and piled beyond an incomplete barrier, undoubtedly constructed by the men in an attempt to seal themselves from the fumes and gases.

Before the bodies were removed, coroners Wadhams and Eno impaneled a group to identify the bodies as they were brought to the surface. The group referred to as "the jury" was comprised of W. J. Harvey, a foreman, Samuel Van Loon, Martin McDonald, James George, Charles Hutchinson, and Thomas Patton. Then began the long, tedious ordeal of bringing each body to the surface.

Mr. Myron Kingsley, who supervised the task, supplied his own horse, windlass, block ropes, and tackles, as well as a crew of men to operate the hoisting apparatus. Removing the bodies was time-consuming. Each time the cage was lifted, the horse pulling the cable traveled in a circle, 5530 feet, more than a mile. Each trip averaged 8 minutes.

As families, friends, relatives, sympathizers, and the merely curious waited, word came from below that sixty-seven bodies were found huddled together. It was later reported that some of the men were in postures of peace, but others denoted signs of struggle and agonizing death. As each body was brought to the surface, an identification was made by the "jury."

While families stood by, the bodies were hoisted to the surface. The newspaper reporter continued to describe the progress in timed reporting: "2:40 p.m. The twenty-fourth corpse is William Reese, Coal Street, Plymouth. Wife in old country. His stepfather and brother were both in the mine; arms raised as though boxing; hands clenched; evidently died in agony. 3:00 p.m. The twenty-sixth body is that of William N. Williams, Plymouth (Turkey Hill) wife and three children; face bloody; wife in crowd screaming."

And so the descriptions continued, a narrative of unending tragedy:

11

"The fifty-second and fifty-third bodies, man with son in his arms. The saddest of all sights today, left arm clasped around the boy John Burtch and John, Jr."

In addition to the sixty-seven bodies found grouped together, others found throughout the mine brought the total to one hundred and ten lives lost in the most devastating single tragedy in a long history of mining holocausts. The victims of suffocation, precipitated by the fire at Avondale were overwhelmingly Welsh, many of them recent emigres. The families of some of those killed were still in Wales waiting for their husbands and sons working at Avondale to send them passage money to the new country.

As the final bodies were brought to the surface, the reporter described the scene.

"Quite a number of people were still here, waiting anxiously for further developments. The burning coal sending blue curling flames, the scores of miners with lamps in their hats, many other men with lanterns flying about, a group of men with lamps at the tunnel. The litter-bearers bringing out their fearful loads of dead humanity, the thick darkness . . . add to this the shrieks of women and crying of strong men."

The news of the Avondale disaster spread throughout the United States and the world. In northeastern Pennsylvania especially, thousands swarmed toward the site of the tragedy. Since the Delaware, Lackawanna and Western Railroad adjoined the mine site, access was easy. By the second day throngs of people numbering over 8,000 made the rescue and recovery difficult. At one point, a water hose was reluctantly used to prevent the crowd from over-running the whole mine yard. Thousands of the throng came from Scranton. From the death list it is apparent that Avondale was as much a tragedy for Scranton as it was for Plymouth. Sixty-one of the one hundred ten victims were residents of Scranton or had had some association with it. The mayor of Scranton, E. S. M. Hill, issued the following proclamation:

Whereas an appalling calamity has occurred in our midst whereby a large number of our citizens perished in pursuit of their legal calling, causing hundreds of heart-stricken orphans, widows and friends to mourn the untimely loss of loved ones;

Now therefore, in view of this terrible affliction, I hereby request the citizens of the city of Scranton to close their respective places of business and keep them closed during the day of the 9th and 10th days of September, instant, that proper respect may be paid to the interment of the remains of the unfortunates.

The Scranton Republican announced that free train rides would be available for persons going to Avondale and returning with the coffins of the killed men. The first train leaving Scranton at 9:30 had ten box cars, nine open flat cars and one passenger car. All were packed full—so full that hundreds of others waiting in Pittston could not board the train. Another train made up of seventeen flat cars and one passenger car was also completely filled. Hundreds unable to find space on either train patiently waited at the station for the trains to return with the victims.

In the meantime, seventy men had started early that morning to dig the graves at the Washburne Street Cemetery in Hyde Park, Scranton. The men in charge were John L. Lewis of Oxford Mine, Thomas Houser of Tripp's Slope and Robert Ruthven, Superintendent of Hyde Park Shaft.

When the trains arrived, the first contingent of the funeral procession proceeded immediately to the cemetery for burial. With the coffins placed in a row, high on the hillside, the Reverend M. A. Ellis read the scripture and the Reverend William Roberts, D.D., delivered the sermon. The message of comfort to the bereaved was introduced by these words:

"This is a sad calamity! A dreadful catastrophe! Death lurking in fire, smoke and sulphur, suffocating and extinguishing the spark of life. Death, insatiate monster: God cannot bribe thee; wisdom cannot elude thee; and tears cannot melt thee. . . . But here we see death . . . in dreadful forms, prostrating men in robust health, in the midst of employment, crushing them . . . without time for reflection, prayer or escape."

The last bodies to be buried at the Hyde Park Cemetery did not arrive until dusk. The day ended and night came as the last long line of twelve coffins and their mourners climbed the cemetery hill at 7 o'clock in the evening.

The tragedy of Avondale led to resolutions of sympathy from Mayor Martin Kalbfleisch of Brooklyn, New York, and from Mayor A. Oakley Hall of New York City. News of the event brought donations from all over the world. The total contributed was $155,000.

The story of Avondale was spread worldwide especially by the *Philadelphia Ledger* and *Harper's Weekly*. The Avondale Disaster still is the most tragic symbol of the dangers of coal mining. Around the world and especially in northeastern Pennsylvania, as long as coal was mined, Avondale was remembered.

Two important legislative reforms resulted directly from the Avondale Fire. Pennsylvania mining laws made it unlawful to build coal breakers directly above the shaft openings and all coal mines were directed to have at least two openings.

Until the 1940's one could still stand on the Avondale hillside, near Plymouth, and see the rubble of pipes, wood, and stone of the shaft and breaker. But today just a short distance from this spot are new, white, modern, split-level homes standing in stark contrast to the black past of Avondale.

The fire at Avondale was the first major disaster of the post-Civil War anthracite era. Two others were to come, the Twin Shaft squeeze in 1896 and the Baltimore Tunnel explosion in 1919. Also to come were hundreds of other accidents for smaller groups of miners and individuals. Explosions, rock falls, fires, and squeezes were common occurrences and marred the lives of miners and their families for almost one hundred years.

The tragedy at Avondale was accepted by most people as an inevitable adjunct of mining. But not by everyone. Among those dissenting was Terence Powderly, a young railroad worker from Carbondale, Pennsylvania. He vowed to raise the conscience of the community to bring safety and dignity to the mining of coal.

Avondale
Disaster
September 6, 1869

Sketches by
Theodore R. Davis
Harper's Weekly

left:
"Bringing up the dead"

below:
"Identifying the dead"

CHAPTER III

An Irish Catholic Builds a Union

Terence Powderly and the Knights of Labor

On September 9th, 1869, a young railroad apprentice living in Carbondale went to the scene of the Avondale disaster. Later he wrote of the experience:

"When on that September day at Avondale, I saw the blackened charred bodies of over one hundred men and boys as they were brought to the surface, I experienced a sensation that I have never forgotten.

"I was just a boy then, but as I looked at John Siney (President of the Workers' Benevolent Association) standing on the desolate hillside at Avondale with his back toward a moss-grown rock, the grim silent witness to that awful tragedy of ignorance, indifference, thoughtlessness, and greed, and listened to his low, earnest voice, I saw the travail of ages struggling for expression on his stern, pale face. I caught inspiration from his words and realized that there was something more to win through labor than dollars and cents for self. I realized for the first time that day that death, awful death such as lay around me at Avondale, was a call to the living to neglect no duty to fellow men.

"John Siney gave expression to a great thought when he said, 'You can do nothing to win these dead back to life, but you can help me win fair treatment and justice for living men who risk life and health in their daily toil.' The thought expressed in that far-away time became my thought. Then, when I listened to John Siney, I could see Christ in his face and hear a new Sermon on the Mount. I there resolved to do my part, humble though it might be, to improve the

17

conditions of those who worked for a living. Of course, I had no plan, the germ of brotherhood was just quickening to life in me, and I had no idea of what I ought to do to help, to be of use to others."

Terence Powderly may not have known exactly what to do, but his instincts took him along the single path of labor organization. Seeing an advertisement in a Philadelphia newspaper about a union meeting, he wrote and asked about a machinist's union. He learned of the Machinist's and Blacksmith's Union with headquarters in Cleveland. Because he could not yet write, he convinced a fellow worker to write for information. An organizer soon arrived in the Scranton area. A local was formed but Powderly, who was 20 years old in 1869, was rejected because of his youth. Later, in November 1871, however, he was accepted and after, as he says, "I learned to write some," he became secretary of the union. His next step was to join the Knights of Labor. The Knights of Labor was less a trade union than a holy mission. As one reads Powderly's autobiography, one can see an Irish Catholic descendant of Hugo Poudrelé, a French Huguenot, building a union on what he deemed to be the practical application of the teachings of Jesus. Powderly was not, however, as many people believe, the founder of the Knights. That honor belongs to Uriah Stephens, a Philadelphia tailor and Greek scholar. Stephens developed the principles and by-laws of the Knights from the National Labor Union of 1866. The Knights of Labor organized in Reading, Pennsylvania, in 1878.

The nature of the organization can best be understood by looking at its literature. Here is what a candidate would hear as he was sworn into the Knights of Labor:

"In the beginning God ordained that man should labor, not as a curse, but as a means of development, physically, mentally, morally, and has set thereunto his seal of approval in the rich increase and reward. By labor is brought forth the kindly fruits of the earth in rich abundance for sustenance

18

and comfort; by labor (not exhaustive) is promoted health of body and strength of mind; labor garners the priceless stores of wisdom and knowledge; it is the 'Philosopher's Stone,' everything it touches turns to gold; 'Labor is noble and holy,' to glorify God in its exercise, to defend it from degradation, to divest it of the evils of body, mind and estate, which ignorance and greed have imposed, to rescue the toiler from the grasp of the selfish is a work of the noblest and best of our race. Without your seeking, without even your knowledge, you have been selected from among your fellows, for that exalted purpose. Are you willing to accept the responsibility and trusting in God and the support of sworn true *****s, labor with what ability you possess, for the triumph of these principles among men?"

The title held by Uriah Stephens, and later by Terence Powderly, was Master Workman. As the Knights welcomed new members, the Master Workman would say in the initiation ceremony:

"On behalf of the toiling millions of earth, I welcome you to this Sanctuary, dedicated to the service of God, by serving humanity. Open and public associations having failed, after a struggle of centuries, to protect or advance the interests of labor, we have lawfully constituted this Assembly. We mean no conflict with legitimate enterprise, no antagonism to necessary capital, but men in their haste and greed, blinded by self-interest, overlook the interests of others and sometimes even violate the rights of those they deem helpless."

The religious accent is apparent. The order had a pattern of secret grips and passwords, not unlike the proliferating lodges, the Masonic orders, the Knights of Columbus, and many other such groups. The procedure for closing meetings included this prayer by the Master Workman:

"Father of all, God of love, we render thee hearty thanks for Thy goodness. Bless all our acts; may all our work begun, continued and ended, redound to Thy glory and the good of man."

19

Each member would then say "Amen" or else repeat the following lines as the meeting ended:

> God of the granite and the rose,
>   Soul of the archangel and the bee,
> The mighty tide of being flows,
>   Through every channel, Lord from Thee,
> It springs to life in grass and flowers.
>   Through every grade of being runs;
> 'Till from creation's radiant towers,
>   Thy glory flames in stars and suns.
> God of the granite and the rose,
>   Soul of the archangel and the bee,
> The mighty tide of being flows,
>   Through all Thy creatures, back to Thee.
> Thus round and round the circle runs.
>   Infinite sea without a shore,
> 'Till men and angels, stars and suns,
>   Unite to praise Thee, evermore.

This prayer was condemned by opponents of the Knights, especially capitalist churchgoers, as pantheistic.

The Knights of Labor in the anthracite region were the heirs of the earliest unions of 1842 and 1848, movements influenced by the English chartists. As we noted earlier, Powderly was converted to the cause of labor by John Siney's speech after the fire at Avondale. Powderly, therefore, brought to the Knights of Labor the heritage of the Workers Benevolent Association of John Siney. Powderly shared and appreciated his view of the need for solidarity among workers: "It had not dawned on us that, in the march of industry, the chasm between the all-round workman and the specialist was opening wider and yet more wide every year. Muscle-saving, brain-impelling machinery was displacing the handicraftsman everywhere and in every line of endeavor. So compelling and rapid were the strides of inventive genius that, even while we were demanding recognition for him who earned his bread through the sweat of his face, the machine was being installed which called for little or no expenditure of sweat. It was ordained perhaps that, in the Knights of Labor, the workers of America should receive their first education in specialization. We admitted all men and taught them the significance and value of organized, cooperative effort. Workers, who up to that time dreamed that their callings could not be classed as skilled, were taught to know that there is no unskilled labor. . . . . All trades, all callings, came into the Knights of Labor, and, catching the inspiration born of touching elbows in a common cause." Membership was open to all except brokers and saloon keepers.

The single most frequently used slogan Powderly invoked in building solidarity among workers was, "An injury to one is the concern of all." But while Powderly believed that labor's strength lay in unity, he did not believe it should take the form of a strike or walkout. Powderly's first opposition to using the strike as a weapon may have been caused by the mine strike of 1871 in Scranton. Just two years after his emotional experience at Avondale, and while still only twenty-two years of age, Terence Powderly moved from his native Carbondale and was employed in the machine shops of the Pennsylvania Coal Company in Scranton. Thus, in the winter of 1871, he was in the middle of a major labor dispute in Scranton.

The strike began when the miners led by the Miners and Laborers Benevolent Association, the new name of John Siney's Workers' Benevolent Association, asked for wage increases plus a promise that wages would not be set arbitrarily without prior notice, as had often happened in the past.

For three months the miners remained unified, but by early spring many miners were destitute and were thinking about a return to work.

The mine owners were ready for action too. During the strike, the owners were unaffected because they had stockpiled coal. But by March, their reserves were running out and they needed to think about the future. The first break in the impasse came when a group of workers agreed to return to work. But when they attempted to enter the mines, they were physically opposed by those miners still on strike. As so often happened, violence began when the strikebreakers tried to go back to their jobs. It reached a climax on Good Friday, April 7, 1871 when a riot involving over one thousand men, some armed with weapons, could not be controlled by police. At the end of the day the striking miners were in control, and the strikebreakers were prevented from working.

The miners won this battle but they lost the war. As a result of the riot, Governor John W. Geary sent in the Pennsylvania National Guard to restore order. These National Guardsmen then were made available to escort willing miners to and from the mines.

With the tide turning, William W. Scranton, superintendent of the Lackawanna Iron and Coal Company, made a dramatic announcement. He opened the Briggs Shaft in West Scranton and promised to escort personally any miner who would return to work. They would, of course, be accompanied by soldiers of the National Guard. Thirty miners accepted Superintendent Scranton's offer.

On May 17, 1871, the miners accompanied by Scranton and nine Pennsylvania National Guard soldiers, were met on their way home by several hundred striking miners and their supporters at Fellows Square, Scranton. When the group began to stone the soldiers and Scranton-led workers, the soldiers retaliated and fired, killing two men, Benjamin Davis and Daniel Jones. Scranton was arrested, taken to the county court house in Wilkes-Barre, and then released on bail. Several weeks later he was tried and acquitted. But the violence on May 17 broke the strike and the miners returned in defeat.

The Knights of Labor continued to organize anthracite workers, but ran into aggressive competition by unions willing to use the strike. One, the Miners National Association of the United States, was formed in 1873, with John Siney, former head of the Workers Benevolent Association, as its president. It reached a peak membership of thirty-five thousand miners before unsuccessful strikes and the conspiracy conviction of its national organizer, Xingo Parks, caused its collapse in 1876. Parks was convicted under a Pennsylvania anti-labor conspiracy law. His crime was, "assisting in the combination of miners for the purpose of raising wages." Siney was also indicted but he was not convicted.

A year later another strike in Scranton, much more bitter and violent, led to another defeat for the miners. The violence climaxed in July 1877. The strike included railroad workers, who were participating in the great national railroad strike of 1877, and miners. The railroad workers capitulated, but the anthracite workers, now organized by a more dynamic union, the Miners National Union, refused to surrender. Once again, violence led to defeat. Incensed by a rumor that William Scranton had written he would soon have the miners working for thirty-five cents a day, the miners gathered three thousand people and went on a destructive rampage. They were finally stopped by a corps of citizen-soldiers, the Scranton City Guard, who shot twenty-eight, killing three and wounding twenty-five. Following the killings, the Pennsylvania National Guard patrolled Scranton for three months. Later, fifty-three of the Scranton City Guard, an organization sanctioned by the Governor, were tried but acquitted of manslaughter.

The decade of the 1870's was a violent one marked by what appeared to be two major defeats for labor organization, that of 1871 and again in 1877. Yet in the midst of these defeats, labor grew stronger. The year 1877, a year of disaster, found Terence Powderly and the Knights of Labor growing to 18,000 members in Luzerne County, which included what today is Luzerne and Lackawanna Counties. The defeats suffered by miners, verified to Powderly that strikes and violence were unproductive.

Even so, competition for membership continued to emerge,

23

this time from a new union of miners called The National Federation of Miners and Mine Laborers of the United States and Territories. Terence Powderly opposed the Federation as a return to trade unionism. He believed labor's strength was in a broad base of labor from all industries. The Knights retaliated by organizing a separate assembly within the structure of the Knights, called the Ntional Trade Assembly 135, to appeal to miners. When William T. Lewis became Master Workman of the National Trade District 135 of the Knights of Labor, he opposed Powderly and joined forces with those who claimed that miners had to fight their own battles and believed in the need for a separate miners' union. Lewis left the Knights, and formed the members of the Federation under a new title, the National Progressive Union of Miners and Mine Laborers of America, really composed of Federation people and using its structure. The Knights group, the National Trade District 135 continued with new officers.

This split in the ranks of the Knights of Labor led to the formation of the United Mine Workers of America. The end of the quarreling and rivalry began in September 1889, when the National Trade District 135 held its annual convention in Wilkes-Barre, Pennsylvania. It was obvious to both the rank and file and to the officers that the only ones benefiting from the union struggle were the mine owners and operators. The Progressive Union came to the same conclusion. Together they issued a call for a joint convention to be held in Columbus, Ohio in January, 1890. The convention turned out to be a momentous one in American labor history. Principles of agreement were adopted and ratified by cheering, arm-waving delegates. The division in labor was healed and the United Mine Workers of America was born on January 22, 1890. The era of the Knights of Labor in the anthracite region came to a close.

Before that, the Knights of Labor had fought against strong opposition from outside as well as inside its organization. In retrospect, the Knights of Labor in the anthracite field were

24

hindered by alleged secrecy. The labor spy Allan Pinkerton called the Knights "an amalgamation of the Mollie Maguires and the Commune." Against such odds, the Knights built a strong membership in the Scranton/Carbondale northern area of the anthracite region. By the summer of 1877, there were 107 assemblies of the Knights in the area with a membership of 15,000. Such a membership accounts in no small measure for the election of Terence Powderly as Mayor of Scranton in 1878.

Powderly saw the Knights' members as potential political reformers as well as unionists. Although only twenty-eight years of age, he knew the ballot-stuffing corruption of the county's political life. Knowing little of currency matters, but much of labor, he became a president of the Greenback Labor Club.[1] The Club called a convention in Pittston and rallied to Powderly's speech: "If we find that the ballot boxes have been stuffed . . . let us hang everyone of them scoundrels. Murder may have been committed in the heat of passion . . . but the man who defeats the will of the people is worse than murderer, burglar, thief, or rapist. He strikes at the foundation of civil government."

In a spontaneous, hard-working, poll-watching campaign, Greenback Labor candidates won a decisive victory and elected the sheriff, recorder, coroner, commissioner, surveyor, and auditor of Luzerne County. The Democrats, who had previously controlled the county, fell behind the Republicans. The extent of the Knight's vigilance was apparent. Powderly described their watch-dog activities: "The ballot boxes from all over the county were taken to the courthouse at Wilkes-Barre for storage and safe-keeping. A detail of one hundred Knights of Labor stood guard around the courthouse from Tuesday, the day of the election, until Thursday when the

---

[1] The Greenback Party was a political party active between 1876 and 1884. Appealing to farmers and laborers, the party advocated the printing of "greenbacks," money to benefit farmers and laborers. The party supported the income tax, women's rights, and other progressive measures.

official count was completed by the judges of the court. Nine hundred other men stood ready throughout Wilkes-Barre to respond to a pre-arranged signal in case of an attempt to enter the courthouse by unauthorized persons. We are determined that there should be no stuffing of ballot boxes. I was one of the hundred to guard the courthouse. I brought a rope with me."

The Greenback Labor Party, which became a power after the election, nominated Powderly for Mayor of Scranton in February, 1878, and he won by a majority of 500 votes against a Democratic-Republican Coalition. He was re-elected in 1880 and again in 1882. In 1882 he declined the nomination for lieutenant-governor of Pennsylvania.

Like America's brightest leaders, Terence Powderly foresaw the needs of his day. In 1878, he urged equal pay for equal work. In September, 1880, on his urging, the Knights of Labor admitted women to its membership. Powderly spoke often with Susan B. Anthony and Elizabeth Cady Stanton. He initiated Frances H. Willard into the Knights of Labor after she visited him at his home in Scranton. Powderly's enlightenment once led to near rioting in Richmond, Virginia, as a result of a speech before the general assembly of the Knights. Powderly stated, "Southern labor regardless of color, must learn to read and write. Southern cheap labor is more a menace to the American toiler than the Chinese, and this labor must be educated." In his lifetime, Powderly was involved in politics, consumerism, and social reform. He wrote that, "In this organization, we were to understand that while we had rights to battle for, we owed duties to our fellow men as well. We could claim no right for self that did not carry with it an obligation and call to do our duty by and to others." One of Powderly's preoccupations was greeted by labor with mixed feelings. He often appeared more interested in temperance than labor. To rank and file members, abstinence was a blue nose interference with personal preference and privilege.

26

Even though Powderly was Master Workman of a powerful, Christian-oriented union, and mayor of the city of Scranton, he ran into opposition from the Catholic hierarchy. The clergy was especially sensitive to any movement hinting of socialism. And, when that movement included secret rituals, it had trouble with the Roman Catholic church.

The Church's opposition to the Knights of Labor reached a climax on May 18, 1878. Terence Powderly was summoned to a meeting between himself, as the mayor of Scranton, and the Bishop of the Scranton Diocese, The Right Reverend William O'Hara. It was a scene reminiscent of the one with Henry IV of Germany kneeling barefoot in the snow before Pope Gregory at Canossa in the Apennine Mountains of Italy in 1077, except that Powderly refused to kneel. Powderly described this sensitive confrontation in his autobiography:

"In May, 1878, I was a delegate to a state convention of the Greenback Labor Party in Philadelphia. I reached my home in Scranton at one o'clock Sunday, May 19. That afternoon, two Knights of Labor friends of mine, James White and John Rinehart, called at my home and told me that (the) Right Reverend William O'Hara, bishop of Scranton, wished to see me at the bishop's residence that evening. I met my friends by appointment and accompanied them to the Episcopal residence.

"On the way to call on the bishop, I asked if they knew why he wanted to see me, but they did not explain. I did not know until after the interview terminated that the bishop had called me out from the altar that morning and had, in effect, excommunicated me by warning the people of the congregation to have nothing to do with me in (the) future." The bishop's words were reported by the national press:

> I warned you against these pernicious secret societies; they are devised by designing men to dupe the unwary and draw them into their toils for the purpose of using them as tools for their own personal advancement. We have one instance of it in this city in a man who has hood-winked the work-

27

ingman into electing him mayor. He is a busybody and a slanderer. He has circulated the rumor that I have approved of one of these secret societies; I have not even considered it. He is a fraud, an impostor, and I warn you against his scheming. Beware of being misled by such a character. Have nothing to do with him!

"That's what the Associated Press carried out of Scranton that evening. Reporters weren't so busy or alert then, or I suppose I would have heard all about it, with variations, before White and Rinehart called me.

"We were admitted to the bishop's reception room where we remained for about a quarter of an hour before he entered the room. After exchanging greetings with the others, the bishop turned to me to make known his reasons for sending for me. I am not trusting entirely to memory, and while this is being rewritten in 1917, it was originally, though more in detail, written within ten days after the occurrence. The bishop asked if my name was Powderly, if I was not the mayor, and, on answering in the affirmative said, 'you are a bad man, a scoundrel; you lied about me and must beg my pardon. Get down on your knees, sir.'

"I was not expecting such a salutation. For a moment I was so confused that I could not think of a word to say. When I at last found my tongue, I said, 'I am not a scoundrel, I did not lie about you, and I shall not beg your pardon.'

"At that the bishop became very angry; he poured on me a torrent of invectives and abuse such as I never listened to before. I am not, and was not then, of angelic temper; never pretended to be. That I spoke warmly in my defense is true, but I mastered my inclination to answer the bishop in kind, and said: 'You sent for me and I came; is it to treat me in this manner you summoned me? If so, we may as well end this meeting now, for I shall not take any more of your abuse.'

"Ignoring my remarks—indeed, he was so angry that I do not think he understood me—he pointed to the floor and

28

said in a most violent manner: 'Kneel down, sir, and beg my pardon for what you have done.'

"I refused to do so, and asked him to tell me what I had done to merit such treatment. His answer was: 'You wrote a letter to West Virginia about me; you lied about me, you slander me, you scoundrel.'

"To that I said: 'I remember writing to a man in West Virginia concerning you, but wrote nothing disrespectful of you.'

"His reply to that was not calculated to place us on a peace footing: 'Yes you did, you slandered me, you lied about me in that letter, you scoundrel, and must beg my pardon. Kneel down, sir.'

"By that time I was very angry, and said: 'I wrote to West Virginia about you; I did lie about you in that letter, for I said you were a kind, just man, and that was a lie, for no man ever used such language to me before. I will not beg your pardon.'

"He then stood up, taking the crucifix which hung at his girdle in his left hand, he raised his right on a level with his forehead and was about to speak when I took a step or two toward him and said: 'Wait, don't do that, you are going to curse me, and I am innocent of any intentional wrong. Do not invoke the image of Him you represent in a wrong. Let me bring you a copy of what I wrote and then, after you read it, if you must curse me, do so. Remember that curses, like chickens, are said to come home to roost. I believe I am right, you can't be sure I am wrong. Don't curse me, but let me show you just what I wrote about you.'

"He lowered the crucifix and, pointing to the door, said: 'Leave my house, sir.'

"Had he been another man, I would have struck him no matter what the consequences might follow. Two valued friends and co-religionists of mine stood by and heard what had transpired. I was humiliated beyond expression, for though I had but recently gone through a political campaign and

29

had been the recipient of unstinted abuse, I had not grown so callous as to receive such treatment and bear it patiently. I answered Bishop O'Hara in this language, and now, after the lapse of thirty-nine years, can see no word or syllable that I would omit:

" 'No, I shall not leave your house, I cannot; it is not your house. My father and mother came to this valley in 1829, and ever since then, they and their children have been paying into the church. In the cathedral across the lot there is money of mine, part of my earnings are in that convent across the street and money of mine is invested in this house. There's not one cent of yours in it; it is not your house; you, sir, are but a tenant here. You weren't known here when this building was erected; you are here as a servant of God. Even though you had a million dollars in it, I'll not stir a foot from it until you retract the abuse you have heaped on my head tonight. Were it a dog I had invited beneath my roof, I would know enough to treat him considerately; you are the most vindictive, unreasoning man I ever met. I'll not leave your house.'

"He turned from me and left the house."

The next day an emissary, the Reverend Dr. Dunn, called on Powderly saying that Bishop O'Hara wanted to see him immediately. Powderly replied by giving to the Reverend Dr. Dunn the Mayor of Scranton's name card with business hours saying, in effect, "If the bishop wishes to see me in my office, I am available." The Reverend Dr. Dunn relayed the bishop's intention of reading him out again the next Sunday. Powderly's answer: "I'll be in my seat next Sunday, and if he uses such language . . . as yesterday . . . I'll proceed . . . in the courts."

The version of the confrontation related by Powderly may have been heavily biased and self-serving; nevertheless, the opposition of the Catholic Church was strong. The archbishop of Quebec, Canada, had condemned the Knights, and the Pope on two occasions had upheld that action.

30

In the lower anthracite region, the suspicions of the Catholic Church about the Knights of Labor led to the organization of the Catholic Workingmen's Society of St. Joseph's Parish in Girardsville, Pennsylvania. Powderly believed the Philadelphia and Reading Coal and Iron Company was an ally in its founding. The preamble of the Catholic Workingmens' Society declared strikes were immoral, that secret societies were a misuse of proper means, and that employers with their sense of justice would pay as high a wage as possible. The president of the Society was the pastor of St. Joseph's Church. The pastor as president prompted Powderly to ask, "Which of the collieries in Girardsville does the pastor of St. Joseph's Church work in?"

The negative stance of the Catholic Church existed until a liberal, more understanding clerical observer of the social and labor scene emerged to change the Church's position. That man was the Most Reverend James Cardinal Gibbons, Archbishop of Baltimore. Cardinal Gibbons presented a convincing paper to the Sacred Congregation of Propaganda in 1887 arguing that the Knights of Labor was secret only in the sense that it was defensively protecting itself against the exploitation of unfair monopolies, that there was nothing in the policies and practices of the Knights of Labor that a Catholic could not share with Church fathers even outside the confessional. He praised Terence Powderly and other officers of the union who had cooperated with him. Cardinal Gibbons saw Powderly as a faithful Catholic, a bulwark against the threat of anarchism and communism.

Cardinal Gibbons, using the encyclical letters of Leo XIII as a guide, wrote his official plea after consulting with the President of the United States, Grover Cleveland, and after hearing Terence Powderly address the Archbishops of the United States. Convinced that Powderly and the Knights of Labor reflected the needs of laboring Catholics, Gibbons described the turbulent social and economic scene in America. He pointed out the danger of alienating the majority of

31

members of the Knights of Labor and the millions of non-aligned laboring men and women. In ringing words he pleaded: "And since it is acknowledged by all that the great questions of the future are not those of war, of commerce . . . but the social questions which concern the improvement of the condition of the great popular masses . . . it is . . . of supreme importance that the Church should always be found on the side of humanity . . . of justice towards the human family." This persuasive plea, delivered in Rome on February 20, 1887, led to a lifting of the ban against the Knights of Labor.

Perhaps Powderly's greatest indirect ally was Leo XIII, a Pope who saw the injustices of the Industrial Revolution and who saw the application of Christian principles by workers, the principles of charity, long-suffering and tolerance, as essential in avoiding industrial warfare.

Powderly regarded himself as a good Catholic and undoubtedly suffered, but he did not surrender to official attacks. He remembered the trying times when his wife sat in her church pew in Carbondale and listened while Father John McGrath warned the congregation of the "fraud from Scranton," Powderly, who will be "soon silenced." "This treatment," Powderly said, "shook my belief in the Church; my faith in the goodness of God was never disturbed." Powderly's faith in the Church was partially restored by the support from friendly pastors. It is obvious that the most frequently used slogan of Powderly and the Knights of Labor had the touch of religious conviction. Terence Powderly rallied laboring men around the slogan, "An injury to one is the concern of all." Using his own compassion, energy, and intelligence, he progressed from a sixteen year old who could not write to an adult admitted to practice law in the courts of Pennsylvania and the Supreme Court of the United States.

Powderly was a middle-of-the-roader, who rejected socialism and the violence associated with the "Molly Maguires." The peak enrollment of the Knights of Labor came after the successful Wabash Strike of 1885, a strike against

32

three of Jay Gould's railroads. Even though in one year the membership of the Knights increased from 80,000 to 700,000, the Knights were reluctant to use the strike as a weapon. The tremendous increase in membership was due also to the support of the governors of Missouri and Kansas who were sympathetic to striking workers. Powderly had great reservations about strikes and believed they were "barbarism."

But the opposition of the Knights to strikes, their accent on progress through reforms such as cooperatives, income tax, the end of child labor, did not answer the cries of the coal miners. Mine workers, plagued by work and family obligations, could not respond to the breadth and idealism of the Knights. Labor leaders and organizations speaking of bread and butter issues—wages and hours—were more appealing. Nevertheless, Terence Powderly paved the way for new leaders and new organizations. Before such a leader could emerge, though, two cataclysmic events occurred—the Twin Shaft disaster of 1889 in Pittston and the Lattimer Massacre near Hazleton in 1897.

Terence Powderly was the greatest Master Workman of the Knights of Labor, the predecessor of the United Mine Workers. He was mayor of Scranton from 1878 to 1884.

CHAPTER IV

An Irish Disaster

Twin Shaft, Pittston, 1896

On Saturday evening June 27, 1896 the residents of the Wyoming Valley retired to sleep as usual. But this was to be no usual night. At 3 o'clock in the morning, Sunday, they were startled as Pittston on the east side of the Susquehanna River and West Pittston on the opposite shore, shook with the vibration and sound of a tumultuous earthquake. Three distinct tremors struck the community. The cause was a massive cave-in or fall of rock and coal in the Newton Coal Company of Pittston. Fifty-eight men were trapped in the mines at Twin Shaft Colliery. Thus, on Sunday morning, June 28, 1896, another milestone was reached in the history of coal mining in the anthracite region.

The names of the victims indicate that this was a tragedy of the Irish, just as Avondale had been that of the Welsh and, as later, the third of the great anthracite disasters at the Baltimore Tunnel in 1919, was that of the Poles, Lithuanians and Slovaks. While other ethnic groups had victims in all the disasters, the predominance of one nationality in each tells us something about the migration into the anthracite area and also of its ethnic composition.

Immediately after the tremor, the Twin Shaft whistle and Pittston fire alarms sounded. In minutes the mine-head was surrounded by hundreds of people, many of them the family members of those working inside the mine. Later, the *Wilkes-Barre Record* described the scene under the headline "A Mine Horror! A Hundred Men Imprisoned in the Twin Shaft. Buried Under a Cave . . . Feared All Are Dead." The article

continued, "Hundreds of people apprehending serious results, none too terrible for their excited minds, rushed to
the Twin Shaft from which the alarm came and found that
the shock so distinctively felt was due to an extensive cave-
in in the sixth or lower vein of that shaft . . .
The fearful and distressing news spread with lightning
rapidity and in a short space of time . . . hundreds of men,
women and children were wringing their hands uttering the
most heartrending cries for loved ones imprisoned in the
dark pit beneath. The hour following the alarm was one long
to be remembered by those witnessing the sight, the anxious
suspense of the workmen, the grief of the families and friends
and the tender sympathy for the afflicted ones by the spectators, requires more than pen can describe.

"Efforts were made to quiet the apprehensions of the grief-
stricken ones by tendering them the little encouragement
possible but unavailing were those efforts put forth as the
mothers, fathers, daughters, sons, sisters and brothers reasonably feared the worst . . . their fears were found to be
well-grounded."

Hope was revived when a few men emerged from the
mine. John Gill was followed by David Richer, Jacob Adams,
and Frank Sheridan. These men had been working near or
at the foot of the shaft and, though blown down by the forces
of the concussion, had been able to ring for the cage. The
sight of these men was most welcome as detailed knowledge
of the catastrophe was unattainable because superintendent
M. J. Langan and mine foreman, Michael F. Lynott, were
both in the mine as were Alexander McCormick, the chief
fire boss, and Thomas Tenpenny, an assistant fire boss.

Those who emerged from the mine described the cause of
the disaster and the attempts to prevent it. It seems that
several days earlier, mine officials had noted movement or
"working" of the strata between the fifth and sixth veins of
the mine. Such movement generally precedes roof falls or
squeezes. Mine officials were concerned, not only because

roof falls were dangerous for the miners and laborers, but also because they disrupted mining operations and the company's profits. Consequently the mine officials pressed into service extra help to put up mine timbers to shore up the roof and to stabilize the sixth vein so the miners could work on Monday morning.

On Saturday night, one newspaper reported, "the orders had gone forth about midnight that as many as possible should be sent down to assist in this dangerous area as the constant cracking and splintering of the roof gave ample indication that the possibilities of danger were most strongly founded." The men working at this point were, "at the foot of No. 3 plane under the flats a little east of Coxton Yards." Responding to orders, a new group of men entered the mine and joined the others between 12 and 1 o'clock Sunday morning.

The four men who first escaped estimated that about one hundred men and their leaders were either trapped or crushed to death. Since the officials were in the mine, there was no complete list of those inside available. Among those known to be inside the mine were: Thomas Garden, John O'Boyle, Anthony Kane, Thomas Murphy, Cornelius Maguire, John McGill, Michael Hughes, James Daly, Michael Connell, John Hart, Michael Gaughan, James Watt, Thomas Watt, Thomas Ruane, and John Kelwe. The names were predominantly Irish. The complete list was released later.

Immediately after the first tremors, the fans inside the mine controlling the air flow throughout the underground workings were turned on with the hope that some air would filter through the caved areas. A rescue team was then enlisted to enter the mine. John Dally, Charles McDonnell and James Leynon were the first to descend. They returned within an hour and reported that the caving was more extensive than anticipated; search parties faced days of dangerous heavy work to remove what appeared insurmountable tons of rock, coal and debris. Two other attempts to find the trapped miners also failed to find a route through another gangway. They reported that there was "havoc everywhere" with passages blocked by pillars, brattice work, air conduits, doors, coal cars, and top rock piled "so promiscuously as to baffle the efforts of any human being to advance."

The rescue attempts were further hindered by the threatened collapse of the unaffected area at the foot of the shaft. The general manager of the colliery, John B. Law, who had been ill at home, now assumed responsibility for the rescue work. He appealed for all available manpower and saw to it that load after load of mine timber was sent down to keep the area at the entrance open. The support held, and fifty men were set to work to clear the way to the main caved area. The job was hindered by fears of seeping gas and explosion, or of the Susquehanna River plunging into the mine—anticipating the Knox Disaster of 1959 by sixty-three years. The Lackawanna River enters the Susquehanna River near Twin Shaft.

The morning of Sunday, July 28, was gloomy and rainy and by noon superintendents and foremen from other coal companies gathered at Twin Shaft to continue their help with the rescue. After consultation, the officials decided to move directly on the main gangway, shoring and supporting the roof as they pressed forward. But movement and cracking in the mine indicated the mine still was in danger of total collapse. Describing the rescue work being done, the state mine inspector was pessimistic, "No, I cannot hold out any more hope and until we find out the extent of the cave-in or have some idea where the men are, we cannot say anything definite. The men, or some of them, may be in an open space with the cave all around them, and, if the fall along the gangway is broken, there is a possibility that we may get at the men in two or three days, but if the fall is extensive all the way, it may take a couple of weeks. . . . There is some gas, but all the men use safety lamps and I have stationed a man at the head . . . to examine the lamps. . . . The greatest danger is from falls at the roof. . . . The weird sounds of all the underground movements would fill the uninitiated with terror but the rescuers are timbering as they go." He reported the crew had gone 900 feet with 900 more feet to go to the area where the main caving had occurred.

At 3 o'clock on Sunday afternoon hope faded that the entombed victims had been somehow sealed off rather than crushed and killed. A number of officials of the Clear Spring mine which adjoined Twin Shaft entered their mine and found no caving. They began knocking on the 100 feet thick barrier which separated the mines of Clear Spring from the works at Twin Shaft hoping for a return signal from trapped men. No return tapping came, leading the rescuers in Clear Spring mine to conclude that indeed the victims had been buried by the collapse.

The Clear Spring venture led to a new plan of proposed rescue. Even though no signal was received, it was decided that cutting through the barrier of 100 feet was faster and easier than working through 900 feet of dangerous caved-in gangway at Twin Shaft. Four shifts of five men were assigned to cut through using diamond drills. A day later the plan was modified because of fear of flooding. The new plan was changed to drill a small bore hole through the 100 foot barrier large enough to make some audible contact.

The heartrending stories told so dramatically in 1869 at Avondale were recalled as newsmen described scenes of pain and suffering and grief. Patrick Hart, an elderly man, waiting for his son, one of the entombed, said, "I have come to be an old man and I took great pride in my son James. He was my only son and he was as good and dutiful a boy as ever breathed. He is down there with the rest and I cannot stand the suspense much longer and I feel as if my heart is breaking." The reporter describes him as an old man with tears, choking with sobs.

Twenty-four hours after the calamity, the rescue teams were working feverishly against insurmountable odds. Further caving, flooding from water seeping in from the Susquehanna River, and the threats of gas were the chief obstacles to progress. The rescue team "with their nerves strung to the highest tension . . . stood and watched the work of hours destroyed in moments." Outside the mine, crews labored incessantly to cut props. The cage rose and descended as fast and as often as it could to supply rescue teams with the huge support logs. Undaunted by setbacks, the rescuers drove on.

For twenty-four hours, wives and children kept vigil with little or no sleep. Typical of those was Mrs. Jim Moran. She waited with her six children, the youngest in her arms. "I wanted Jim to get out of the mines," she said, "and get something else to do. He tried to please me but he could get no work and he kept on going down every day there was anything to do. I couldn't sleep a wink last night and I and the little ones sat at the windows waiting for Jim to come home. . . . We have been here since this morning." Mrs. Moran was just one of many wives and children. "There was no demonstrative sorrow—The shrieks, the loud wailing and the piercing cries that followed the first gathering . . . were past," reported an observer.

The children involved indirectly in the disaster numbered over one hundred. Mr. J. Langan, 43 years of age, the superintendent, was the father of ten children. Michael F. Lynott, the mine foreman, was the father of seven. The fire boss, Alexander McCormick, was the father of nine. One hundred and one children were left fatherless.

By Tuesday, June 30, 1896, the number of men entombed was listed as "fifty Americans and twenty-five foreigners." Representing the common prejudice of the day, the "Americans" were those who spoke English without an Eastern European accent. The all-inclusive term used in the press to describe "foreigners" was usually "Polander" describing anyone from Poland or the Austria-Hungarian Empire.

The newspapers of July 3, announced that Governor Hastings had appointed a committee of mine inspectors to try to determine the cause and future prevention of such accidents. The investigation was to begin at noon on July 6.

During the next week the laborious and dangerous attempt to clear the massive fall continued with three shifts of men working around the clock. The work moved slowly, sometimes just 20 feet in a whole day. As the first emotions and spirit of cooperation faded, controversial opinions began to emerge about earlier mining at Twin Shaft: charges of unsafe mining procedures, of improper timbering and propping, and of ignoring signs of squeezing and caving weeks before the disaster. Even the appointments of the Governor were criticized as being dominated by the coal company.

By this time, the newspapers speculated and confirmed what the people of Pittston had been discussing on the street, that the herculean task of finding the men or their bodies was an impossible one. Three shifts of men were now moving only fifteen feet a day. Recovery, it was estimated, would take two months. If the men had scattered into different parts of the caved acreage, finding all the bodies might take over a year. The company hinted that it would discontinue the search and put the money they were using for recovery into a relief fund for families of the victims.

Discontent also was growing among the work crews. They were being paid $1.50 to $2.00 a day. At the outset they had volunteered out of compassion for fellow workers. Now they were paid less for harder and more dangerous work than their regular employment, and the hope of saving their friends was passing.

The hope of the Clear Spring entry had faded too. The drilling at the adjacent colliery of Clear Spring was abandoned when it was concluded that the entombed men were approximately one mile from where the drilling had begun. The earlier suggestion adopted in the first days of the disaster had turned out to be less than practical and was discontinued.

It became apparent that the men in the mine on Sunday

41

knew of the danger. The events just prior to the accident were recounted by Edward Hughes, one of those men who refused to stay in the mine. He stated that there were about 45 men on the 7:30 Saturday night shift. Because of an earlier explosion and gas they were prevented from starting their work which was to timber and support the roof. Hughes continued: "While we waited . . . the crackling grew worse. Finally, John Williams got up and proposed we go home. 'Boys,' he said, 'the best thing we can do is get out of here.' Martin Haley suggested we throw up a stone and decide whether to go or stay. They did so to a chorus of mixed calls of wet and dry. The stone turned up wet and four started out." Hughes is quoted as saying, "I expected all would go out when the start was made but poverty will often make a man do things he knows is not the best for him, especially in these hard times." After they left the mine, the men met some of the bosses re-entering and two of the emerging men were persuaded to return. Six timbermen who had been working outside also joined the inside crew. Edward Hughes continued to his home.

The investigation ordered by Governor Hastings began on July 10. The hearings were held in St. Aloysius Hall with the Attorney General of Pennsylvania in charge. The purpose of the investigation, according to the Attorney General, was to determine whether state mining laws had been obeyed, whether there was company or personal negligence, and what, if any, new legislation might prevent future tragedies like Twin Shaft. The families of the victims were represented by E. F. McGovern of Wilkes-Barre and W. H. Gillespie and P. A. O'Boyle of Pittston. The Newton Coal Company, owners of Twin Shaft, were represented by attorneys J. B. Woodward and F. W. Wheaton of Wilkes-Barre.

The first witness called was Edward Hughes who testified that the mine had been unsafe for six months, that the gangways were too wide, and the coal pillars left as support were too weak.

The mine inspector, Mr. McDonald in charge of inspecting the Twin Shaft Colliery for the state testified next that the cave area was not 8 or 10 acres but 200 acres. He noted that he checked Twin Shaft Colliery only a few times a year because his responsibility included 45 breakers and 65 other collieries. He reported that gangways were 12 to 25 feet wide and stated the law does not dictate the size of coal pillar support. McDonald deemed the ones at Twin Shaft were strong enough. He had not been informed, he said, of the squeeze situation in the mine but admitted he did observe a break or fissure that had been repaired. Mr. Hughes, re-called to the stand, reported the fissure was large enough to put his arm in, and that he had reported it and observed it with the mine foreman. The questioning aimed at mine in-spector McDonald brought the other mine inspectors, now acting as investigators to his defense. Asked outright of his opinion as to the cause of the Twin Shaft disaster, mine inspector McDonald stated in his opinion, theoretical of course, that the cause was the geologic movement of Campbell's Ledge, a huge promontory or cliff rising above the Sus-quenhanna River.

The hearings continued for a week with conflicting testi-mony, indicating on the one hand negligence and unsafe mining, and on the other hand, lawful, efficient, and safe mining. Most of the questions and answers centered around methods of propping, anticipating caving, the control of gas, the possibilities of gas explosions, and the extent, dimen-sions, and locations of coal pillars. The effects of water and dangers of overhead rivers and streams also were subjects of discussion. Occasionally a speaker in the audience would harangue the officials with accusations. Frequently the hear-ings became tense.

The Commission appointed by Governor Hastings re-leased its report to the public on September 25, 1896, three months after the Twin Shaft caving disaster. The Commis-sion, made up of mine inspectors William Stein, Edward

Roderick, and Edward Brennan, exonerated mine inspector McDonald. They observed, however, that the superintendent, who lost his own life had made a fatal error. Rather than using the customary practice of shoring up from the stabilized areas and gradually moving toward the unstable sections, the superintendent went directly to the middle of the weakest part of the mine roof with his men and attempted to prop it and stabilize it. They also speculated that the character of the squeeze convinced them that an explosion had occurred. They went on to describe characteristics of mining in the colliery, all of which had been previously supported or denied.

Since one of the main purposes of the commission was to suggest ways of avoiding similar tragedies, it made the following recommendations:

1) That pillars of coal should be retained in the mine and left standing in such numbers as to provide safety.
2) When two seams of coal are mined, pillars should support both seams. Exceptions would be by permission of mine inspectors. The robbing of these pillars would be permitted if they did not jeopardize the surface.
3) All maps showing air currents and workings should be provided to inspectors. The absence of maps had impeded rescue operations at Twin Shaft.
4) Safety lamps should be used. Open lamps were condemned but not prohibited.

As one reads the recommendations of the commission and recalls the history of mining from the Twin Shaft Disaster to the Knox Disaster of 1959, it is interesting to observe how frequently the recommendations of the commission have been ignored. The absence of maps, the robbing of pillars so as to cause surface subsidence, the inadequate information supplied by mine inspectors, and general violations of safety

44

have characterized the anthracite coal industry throughout its history.

The outcome of the hearing was eagerly awaited by many. However, to the wives, children, and families of the fifty-eight men whose bodies were never recovered, the report seemed an academic exercise, cold and unrewarding. For the families of victims there was no Workmen's Compensation. A relief fund was organized and contributions from throughout Pennsylvania raised $80,000 and distributed it to the families of the victims.

The Twin Shaft tells us of the excruciating trauma found in the mining of anthracite coal. It accents the personal and emotional suffering often lost in the writing of economic history. The Avondale fire projected Terence Powderly forward in the Knights of Labor. The Twin Shaft tragedy was the first of two events which together produced another labor giant, John Mitchell. The second event was the Lattimer Massacre, a year after Twin Shaft in 1897.

Up to the time of the tragedy, the Twin Shaft had a relatively good safety record. Only nine fatalities were recorded between 1889 and 1895, a period when 1,994,623 tons of coal were produced. A detailed geologic study of the mine described in an article in the *Colliery Engineer and Metal Miner* did not reveal a specific cause for the collapse. One theory suggested that mining up to the controversial fissure caused the heavy strata to sag and ultimately break.

The deteriorating remains of the Twin Shaft Colliery (about 1952) reveal little to indicate the tragic squeezes of Sunday morning, June 28, 1896. The bodies of 58 victims, most of whom were Irish, were never recovered.

This view of the impenetrable barriers created by a mine squeeze illustrates the obstacles facing rescuers at the Twin Shaft disaster. The official is Ivor Williams of Nanticoke.

CHAPTER V

A Massacre of Eastern European Miners

Lattimer, 1897

The wave of migration which first brought the Welsh, Irish, German, Scotch, and Scotch-Irish to the anthracite region of northeastern Pennsylvania and later the Polish, Slovaks, Lithuanians, Russians, and Italians, changed the anthracite region and made it an ethnic mosaic similar to New York, Philadelphia and Chicago. In each area, ethnic ignorance and rivalries produced prejudice and sociological turmoil. The established and the establishment were distrustful and prejudiced by the appearance, strange languages, and culture of the late-comers. No better example of this distrust is found than that revealed by the infamous Lattimer massacre, a labor catastrophe and personal tragedy of some magnitude, often ignored in labor history.

A small mining patch, Lattimer Mine, was founded in 1869, the year of the Avondale disaster. In 1897, Lattimer was just another coal patch whose center was the colliery and the breaker. Although its first residents were predominantly Welsh, by 1897 Lattimer was populated mostly by Italian laborers, and the surrounding coal towns were predominantly Slavic.

Like all small coal patches in the Hazleton area, Lattimer could attribute its life to the discovery of coal, to the initiative of men like Ario Pardee who, before the Civil War, saw the potential for coal, and especially to George Markle for his improvements to the coal breaker.

Lattimer and the surrounding patches were festering on

September 10, 1897. The miners were tired of the prejudice and bigotry. They had had enough of the oppressive "boss-ism" of foremen and superintendents like Gomer Jones who were intent on establishing "discipline" among the "hun-kies," all in the name of efficiency and management. They were disgusted at the requirement that they buy in company-owned stores at inflated prices. These were causes for revolt. Instead labor organization developed with attempts to bring about reforms.

An awareness grew among immigrants like Mary Septak, who saw exploitation and cruelty with an intelligent and compassionate eye, and hoped to give dignity and direction to the hopes and purposes of the working men. An orga-nization came in the form of the United Mine Workers. The new immigrants who worked and lived in Lattimer were inspired by Mary Septak as they listened to her speak in their own native tongues about the new United Mine Workers. Formed on January 22, 1890, the new union was just seven years old. It promised the end of coal company exploitation and economic injustice. And yet, though the miners were imbued with new hope and strengthened leadership, their adversary, the coal companies, still controlled the political and police power of the communities.

The immediate cause of the Lattimer labor dispute was the discharge of twenty young mule drivers at the Honey-brook Colliery in McAdoo. A new order directed the drivers to care for the mules at the end of their shifts, and to see that they were returned to their stables. The stable work was to be done without pay. When the drivers refused to obey this new order, they were discharged by the company division superintendent, Gomer Jones, a recent appointee who had vowed to bring order and discipline to the collieries under his jurisdiction.

On August 14, the mule drivers retaliated to their dis-charge with a picket line. Soon, over two thousand other mine workers were involved.

An altercation between Jones and the pickets incensed the already aroused mule drivers, laborers and miners. Jones, frequently called "The Slave Driver," attacked one of the pickets, John Bodan, with a crowbar. The rash act almost cost him his life as the pickets jumped on him to support Bodan.

From August to September 10, the small mining communities near Hazleton—Audenreid, McAdoo, Harwood, Cranberry, Beaver Brook, Jeansville, Lattimer, Harleigh, and Ebervale, all lived in a state of agitation. The organizing efforts of the new United Mine Workers' representative, John Fahy, the activities of unaffiliated leaders, and the minor outbreaks of violence made the late summer weeks troublesome ones.

On August 17, 1897, a delegation representing the aggrieved miners from McAdoo met with Elmer H. Lawall, the top official of the Lehigh and Wilkes-Barre Coal Company in Hazleton. Lawall cancelled the work orders of Gomer Jones, but refused to punish Jones. He promised that a wage increase would be considered, but not until the men returned to work.

The disappointed grievance committee took the report to Mahalchick's Hall in McAdoo. Their report left hundreds of miners dissatisfied and angry over the specific Jones issue plus the old festering dissatisfactions involving the company stores, wages and working conditions.

On September 1, 1897, a formal strike vote of the miners employed in various collieries of the Lehigh and Wilkes-Barre Coal Company set off ten days of turmoil, culminating in the historic massacre of September 10. Those who sympathized with the miners described the marching and rallying as "patriotic." Opponents labeled these activities as the mulling of "foreigners" and "agitators," and "a reign of terror."

Hundreds of miners attempted to expand the strike in lower Luzerne and Carbon Counties. Their objectives were to achieve solidarity, to close the mines, to eliminate scabs, to unionize the industry, and once and for all, to wipe out the oppression and exploitation. Mine owners and many others, including the *Wilkes-Barre Times*, saw the actions of the miners as an attack on private property and community values. On the other hand, the *Hazleton Daily Standard* sympathetically called on the operators to "meet the men halfway, and the trouble . . . will be a thing of the past."

John Fahy continued to organize the miners. The membership enrollment fee was thirty cents, a sum significantly difficult for family men with children making two or three dollars a week. But Fahy soon had eight thousand union members, and they moved forward, praising the capitalist system, calling for understanding and fairness for capital and labor.

Management was also organizing. Using the Pennsylvania Riot Act of 1860 as a rationale, the mine owners and others convinced Sheriff James L. Martin of Luzerne County to post a public notice throughout the strike area referring to "acts of disorder . . . men forcibly prevented from pursuing their daily avocations," and giving notice to "refrain from unlawful assembly" and warning that "lawlessness . . . will be punished. . . ."

To implement his directive, Martin deputized eighty-seven men, most of them with Anglo-Saxon names. Many of the deputies were the professional men of the community and owed their income and livelihood to some coal-related occupation. They were issued Winchester rifles and shells.

During this period, delegations of miners, usually in great numbers, marched from colliery to colliery, getting others to strike in a show of solidarity. The one colliery still in operation was Lattimer. There were several reasons for this. First, Lattimer was two miles north of the strike zone, which was concentrated in the area south of Hazleton. Secondly, Lattimer was not a Lehigh and Wilkes-Barre Coal Company mine. Lattimer was a Pardee colliery as was Harwood. But the Harwood miners had joined the strike and were eager

51

to convince the Lattimer men to join them. As long as the breaker at Lattimer was working and the mine was open, the Pardee Coal Company had a place to process coal and a wedge for reopening the mines already closed. This situation was understood by the miners and union officials. In their eyes, the Lattimer Colliery had to shut down. Evidently, the men working at Lattimer were sympathetic. They sent word that if the men from Harwood Mine, two miles southwest of Hazleton, marched to Lattimer six miles away the men of Lattimer would respond; they would walk out and join the strike. The men of Harwood responded with enthusiasm, remembering, however, the orders of John Fahy, of the United Miner Workers, not to carry clubs or anything that would be interpreted as a weapon. Marchers were ordered to carry only the American flag.

On September 10, 1897, an unseasonably hot day, four hundred miners and laborers set out to close the Lattimer mine. During the first week of the strike, Sheriff Martin and his posse had been successful in their intimidation, but as the four hundred men from Harwood arrived at McKenna's Corners in West Hazleton, the rebellion of the miners and the frustration of a posse tired of policing the "hunkies," resulted in pushes, curses, threats and a few punches. Some members of the posse were filled with disdain for the foreigners whom they saw as an un-American alien influence, desecrating pure America. They had been aching for days to get a hand on some "Polack" heads.

At McKenna's Corners, a confrontation was prevented by the intercession of the chief of police of West Hazleton, Evan Jones. He declared that the miners had a right to march if they agreed to by-pass Hazleton and march on the perimeter through undeveloped fields and paths. The marchers agreed. When they resumed marching, the posse boarded streetcars to take them from West Hazleton through Hazleton to Lattimer. While most of the coal patches in the eastern middle coal field were isolated settlements of clapboard company houses, a circuitous streetcar track touched some of them and provided transportation to Hazleton and West Hazleton.

By the time the protesting miners arrived in Lattimer at 3:00 p.m., the posse was waiting with loaded rifles. From this point on, descriptions of the events were colored by the sympathies of the witnesses. However, witnesses to the Friday masacre agreed that Sheriff Martin, with the posse at his back, moved forward toward the marchers. Martin supposedly clicked his revolver but it did not fire. Whether the sheriff ordered, "fire," or whether the members of the posse seeing the miners surrounding the sheriff as they passed by him, acted on their own and opened fire, was later to be argued in court. Regardless, in the next few minutes, the shooting began and Lattimer was impressed in America's labor history.

Eight of the marching miners were killed instantly. Thirty-nine were seriously wounded, and eleven of them died later. Altogether, sixty miners were shot. The streetcars that just an hour before had brought the sheriff and his deputies to Lattimer were later loaded with dead and wounded for the Hazleton hospital. Nineteen miners lost their lives in a bloodbath which has often been ignored in the history of labor violence.

The Hazleton community was in turmoil; some feared a mass uprising of miners and reprisals; others were ashamed, indignant, and grief-ridden. A public mass meeting at Donegal Hill baseball field heard a Protestant minister call for cool heads until the guilty were punished. Other leaders, speaking in Slovak, Polish and German united in a display of ethnic unity seldom seen at the time.

The public learned that those massacred—the editor of the *Hazleton Sentinel* was to lose his job for headlining the tragedy as a massacre—were real people and family men, and not just "weird hunkies."

John Nemeth, a prosperous Hazleton merchant who had once been a breaker boy, was involved in handling immi-

gration for steamship companies. An Hungarian, he befriended the new arrivals from the Austro-Hungarian Empire and tried to make known to the Hazleton community
the good qualities of the immigrants. Nemeth contacted the
Austro-Hungarian Imperial Government through their Con-
sul General Theodorovitch in Philadelphia. He, in turn, advised their ambassador in Washington to present the matter
to the American Secretary of State.

On the afternoon of the shooting, Nemeth rode horseback
to Harwood and saw bloodied victims and their hysterical
families. He stayed there until late in the evening, then at
midnight rode back to Hazleton where he encountered a
Wilkes-Barre Times reporter. Eager to get the story national
attention he told the reporter that Austria-Hungary would
undoubtedly take action on the killing of its citizens, saying,
"The killing of the Hungarians is a matter of some moment
to the United States Goverment." Behind the statement was
the knowledge that in New Orleans in 1891, the killing of
eleven Italians by an aroused mob precipitated talks of re-
taliation by the Italian government. The United States later
indemnified the families of the victims of the New Orleans
killings.

The action of John Nemeth and the community concern
of church leaders and union officers required an accountability. Against their wishes, the National Guard was sent
into the area, tagging the community with a lawless image.

The atmosphere in Hazleton in the days following the
shootings was described as "an unnatural quiet." There were
sadness and despair in the community, but also a seething
discontent. The quiet was maintained by a group of Philadelphia City Troops, and a battalion of the Eighth Regiment
under General John Gobin. Attempting to help the resto-
ration of peace, a body of priests and ministers met with the
General and interpreted the views of the people of the battered community. Mayor Altmiller ordered saloons closed
until 4 p.m. Underneath the calm, there was a demand for

THE BREAKER
WHISTLE BLOWS

the arrest of the deputies, and a continuation of the strikes.

Warrants for the arrest of the deputies had been approved by Squire Gorman, but General Gobin stopped their serving. Actually, Sheriff Martin was the general's superior in this situation. Gobin, responding to a reporter's questions, explained his position. "He (Sheriff Martin) is my superior. . . . To arrest him would be like arresting the commanding officer of an army in time of war. It shall not be done while I am here and while public feeling runs so high."

The correspondent asked, "What would you do if Sheriff Martin were arrested in some outlying towns while on his way to Hazleton?"

"What would I do? I'd send a squadron of cavalry after him and bring him back quicker than h—l."

A labor leader, hearing of General Gobin's remarks, stated, "We have our heads in the lion's mouth. No attempts will be made to serve the warrants until peace is restored and the troops have left. Then the law will take its course."

On Monday, September 13, funerals were held for 12 of the victims. Despite the general's orders that no bands were to participate and that no flags nor arms were to be displayed during the service, the procession was described: "The various Polish, Hungarian, Lithuanian, and Italian organizations marched to the slow music of bands. The ceremonies were touching . . . and those who witnessed them could not but marvel at the self-control displayed by men who . . . were said to be beyond control." General Gobin kept his soldiers from the funeral sites.

Evidence that there were some who saw the miners in other than the stereotyped mold is also apparent from this newspaper report.

"Let me tell you, there is a great deal more under the surface in this affair than people imagine. To say that these foreigners have no organization, that each man acts on his own free will. I do not think this is true. . . . I tell you these men have learned to organize and are better organized than

English-speaking people have any idea of. No, this is not a leaderless mob."

In the meantime, the new organizer in the area, John Fahy, called for collective bargaining. "In my opinion, if the proper thing were done, operators and miners would come together and agree upon a uniform scale of wages and conditions . . . fair to employer and employed."

But the image of infuriated foreigners, of wild Hungarians persisted. The "Audenreid Outrage," of Thursday, September 9, had occurred when a group wrecked the home of Gomer Jones, Superintendent of the Lehigh and Wilkes-Barre Colliery in Audenreid. The men involved also stole a quantity of explosion powder, and allegedly ransacked the Audenreid company store. These and other violent incidents incited fear within the communities.

By Tuesday following the Lattimer tragedy, it was reported that the Lehigh and Wilkes-Barre Company had settled with its men. This news apparently encouraged men in other collieries to make some demands.

Three Coxe Brothers and Company's collieries, one on Buck Mountain, one at Eckley, and one at Oneida employed a total of 1200 men, 300 of whom were at Eckley. On September 13, trouble had broken out at Eckley. Two hundred miners at Buck Mountain went on strike and started toward Eckley, 3 miles away. The superintendent at Eckley asked General Gobin for troops but later withdrew this request, believing the marchers had stopped. In the meantime the marchers reached Eckley in the afternoon. A dispatch reported the working miners had been roughly handled by the striking miners from Buck Mountain.

The strike spread throughout the Coxe mining operations. About 2,000 men employed at the No. 7 Colliery demanded a ten percent increase. There were between 5,000 and 7,000 men employed by the Coxe Company. The pay demand was based on the lower scale of wages at Coxe Collieries. The company store was not declared an issue.

In the days following the tragedy, the Lattimer Massacre unified Eastern European miners. In Shenandoah, south of Hazleton, a mass meeting of 4,000 Lithuanians, Poles, Hungarians and Slavonians was held on the property of the Lithuanian church with the Reverend Peter Abromallis presiding. His curate, the Reverend J. Milukas assisted. The resolution of this group and other ethnic religious bodies revealed the unity and strength of the new immigrants.

The unity was very visible in the high requiem masses celebrated in the Polish, Lithuanian and Slovak Roman Catholic churches and also the Greek Catholic denominations throughout the Hazleton and Shenandoah areas.

For many months many felt that there never would be any accountability for the Lattimer killings. The posse, composed of community establishment members was considered to be the enforcer of law and order and immune from prosecution. However, the persistence of a minority prevailed, so that finally on February 1, 1898, a cold winter day, the trial began in Wilkes-Barre.

Presiding was Judge Stanley Woodward. The prosecuting lawyers seeking justice for the Lattimer victims were James Martin, District Attorney, John McGahren, John T. Gorman and James Scarlet. Defending the posse was Henry W. Palmer, who had been the attorney general in Pennsylvania (1879–1882), George Ferris, and John T. Lenahan.

The jury was composed of the following: Eli Weaver, Plymouth, laborer; D. R. Shaw, Ross Township, carpenter; Albert Follman, Wilkes-Barre, ropemaker; Alfred Stevens, Wilkes-Barre clerk; Herman Gregory, Huntington Township, farmer; Ada Laroon, Sugarloaf, tinsmith; C. C. Ransom, Plymouth, housebuilder; B. M. Rood, Bloomingdale, farmer; Jones B. Oxrider, Carbon, carpenter; H. H. Wolfe, Ross Township, farmer; and, A. Washburn, Freeland, carriage maker. There was not one miner or mine laborer on the jury. None were ethnically identifiable with the victims. All the jurors were Protestant and Republican.

57

For the prosecution, representing the workers, the most difficult challenge was to overcome the restrictions imposed upon them by the indictment. The indictment against the deputies was confined to one person, the murder of Michael Cheslak. The allegation made all the deputies defendants. The prosecution had to prove that the workers marched in a peaceful manner, that they were unarmed, and that the deputy sheriffs killed one man, Michael Cheslak, with malice and premeditation.

The case for the marching mine strikers was constantly interrupted by the altercations between Gorman, attorney for the mine workers and their families, and Lenahan, attorney for the accused deputies. At one point Gorman said, "We know the law."

"If that is so," replied Lenahan, "it is the only law you ever knew and I further say that you are a low down puppy and you don't know who your father is."

Gorman walked to Lenahan's table and raised his fist.

"You dare hit me and I'll kill you, you coward," screamed Lenahan.

Such language and behavior mixed with the spectator outbreaks of approval and disapproval marked the days of the trial.

Here is the passionate plea of John McGahren as he desperately sought justice for the miners and their families:

"Gentlemen of the jury, we will show you facts that will make this shooting a disgrace to civilization. We will show you how these men were lined along the sides of the road with sixteen-shooter rifles. The Sheriff came out again at Lattimer with a revolver in his hand. He was told they were on a peaceful mission, but the Sheriff grabbed one of them by the neck and pointed his pistol in the man's face. He snapped his pistol in his face several times and finally it went off and shot the man in the head. The man who carried the American flag was the first to be shot down. Price, one of the deputies, stepped out and the others called, 'Come back

58

or we will shoot you, too.' Then there were two shots and the strikers began to run. Then the deputies began firing at the unarmed, fleeing men. It was a horrible massacre, gentlemen. The deputies continued firing for five minutes at the fleeing men, and some of the deputies ran up on the railroad tracks to get a good aim. One man had five bullet wounds in his head. We will show you that nineteen men were killed, thirty-five injured; many of the latter will carry wounds to their graves, crippled for life. And we will show you, gentlemen, that most of these men were shot in the back, while they were running away. All this under the eyes of the Sheriff, who should protect these poor fellows. Why, gentlemen, it was worse than an Indian massacre of our early settlers when there was no law. And, after the shooting, the horrified residents ran to give aid and water to the men while the deputies stood about smoking cigars. Another man found a bleeding, dying fellow lying in the woods crying for water. The man met Hess, a deputy, and asked how he could do such butchery, and the latter raised his gun and said, 'Shut up, or I will shoot you, too.'

"The school teacher, Miss Coyle, saw the first shot and thought it was a blank cartridge, but she saw the man fall, and the other teacher, Mr. Guscott, said, 'My God, don't you see the men falling! They are being shot!' and then a bullet went through the window of the school, breaking four window panes." The summation ended fifteen days of testimony for the mine workers. Much of it was given by victims still bandaged. The defense, Attorney Henry W. Palmer, saying the testimony was tedious and repetitious arose to concede that there had been a march, that the men were unarmed and that they had been fired on and many wounded and killed. The admission shocked the court and spectators. Palmer, however, had his defense well planned. He wanted to get to the point that his clients were acting in self-defense to protect the community.

The defense for Sheriff Martin's posse had a less complicated task. Their purpose was to demonstrate that a state of riot existed, that representing law and order the posse was doing its duty. Furthermore if they had committed questionable acts, they had done so under extreme provocation or in self-defense.

The case of the defendants, the Sheriff's posse, was presented by George S. Ferris rather than the emotional John T. Lenahan. Ferris began in a calm rational way saying, "the story of the Lattimer riot has never yet been told.

"We shall show you that during the week prior to the Lattimer shooting, acts of riot and outrage were of more than daily occurrence. The reign of the law had given place to a reign of terror. The highways were swept by surging masses of armed and desperate men. Peaceful citizens were forced into their ranks. Those who resisted were set upon, beaten, clubbed and wounded . . . some of them nigh unto death. Those who fled from the fury of the mob were pursued, stoned, and fired upon. The sanctity of the home was violated. Dwelling houses were broken into and men dragged out of them—or forced to flee to the woods for their lives. Women were assaulted and threatened with death. Robbery was committed. Buildings were attacked and windows smashed with stones; collieries were taken by storm. Men who sought to earn an honest living were driven from their work. The whole community was terrorized. The local authorities were powerless; and law had been supplanted by anarchy. This is no fancy sketch, gentlemen; what I tell you here the witnesses will tell you there (the witness box) and more. But neither I nor they have language to express the horrible anxiety and paralyzing fear in which those people lived.

"Such was the condition of affairs when the Sheriff arrived upon the scene. He was at Atlantic City when he heard the call to duty, but, like the faithful officer and brave man that he is, he at once obeyed the call. He arrived at Hazleton on Monday, September 6. On the way, he had telegraphed the sheriffs of Carbon and Schuylkill counties, in which like depredations had occurred, to meet him in Hazleton. They did so. The three sheriffs published their proclamations, together with the law relating to riots, in the first issue of the local newspapers, and also by handbills posted in conspicuous places throughout the region. These proclamations called upon all people to keep the peace and refrain from all acts of violence and lawlessness. On the same evening, Sheriff Martin selected his posse. He did not choose loafers, bar-room bummers, toughs and thugs, but chose good, law-abiding citizens, men of good judgment, good character, good standing in the community.

"Sheriff Martin addressed his posse: 'Our mission here is to keep the peace and protect life and property. You are to take your orders from me. Under all circumstances keep cool and don't get excited. You are not to fire at any one except in two cases. First, when I order you to fire, which I will do at the proper time, if present and able to give the order, and second, in an emergency when I am either absent or unable to give the order, you must exercise your own judgment. If you see my life or your own in danger, then fire.'

"From and including September 2, to and including September 10, the acts of riot and outrage which I have mentioned were of more than daily occurrence. They occurred at Yorktown, McAdoo, Silver Brook, Jeansville, Hazleton No. 1, Cranberry, Harwood, Cuyle's Strippings, Harwood a second time, Crystal Ridge, Ebervale, Lattimer, Hazleton Shops, Crystal Ridge a second time, Little Beaver Meadow, Harwood, Crystal Ridge a third time, West Hazleton and Lattimer a second time. I shall not attempt to rehearse the details of this riot. You will hear from the witnesses who saw them with their own eyes, and can tell you of them far better than I. But, as having special bearing upon the final attack by the mob on the 10th, I may say that at the riot at Lattimer on Tuesday, the 7th, the mob fired their revolvers but were dispersed by the deputies stationed there by a few shots fired over their heads. As they left, they shouted back at the deputies: 'You s—— of b————! You got us this time, but tomorrow we'll get you with five thousand men.'

"The plan for the final attack on Lattimer was consummated at two meetings held the night of Thursday, September 9—one at Harwood, the other at Cranberry. At both, the presence of the Sheriff and his duty to preserve the peace and prevent acts of violence and intimidation were fully known. One of the Sheriff's proclamations was posted in plain sight near the schoolhouse where the Harwood meeting was held. It was read by some of the crowd who understood English and by them translated to the others. At Cranberry, a procession headed by a drum and a flag paraded the streets shouting out the order that all men must march to Lattimer the next day to stop the mines. We shall prove to you, that if on the morrow the Sheriff had interfered with them, they had threatened that they would blow him up, and that they would then give the deputies the same dose; and they had in their possession revolvers that would do the business. We shall show you further that the men at Lattimer had no grievance, did not wish to strike, and did wish to continue at work. On the following day, the memorable 10th of September, the mob gathered at Harwood. It was made up of men from that place and from Humboldt. When they reached Lattimer, they were six to eight hundred strong.

"They were armed with clubs, iron bolts, bars and revolvers. They freely announced their purpose to be to march upon Lattimer and stop the works. They were warned not to go there, as bullets might be flying. The reply was, 'we no 'fraid—we got bullets, too!' They said to men whom they ordered to join them, 'If you want revolvers, we'll get them for you.' They expected to be joined by the desperate McAdoo crowd who had terrorized that whole region on the previous Friday. The McAdoo men failed to come and the others, growing impatient of delay, set out upon their desperate errand. From the start, they spread terror wherever they went. They rushed from house to house in Harwood and Cranberry, breaking into them and dragging men out of them and forcing them into their ranks, beating and wounding those who resisted and stoning and firing upon those who fled. The rioters threatened to dash out the brains of a heroic woman who stood on the floor of her own home with a loaded gun in defense of her husband, who was hiding from them in the cellar. They fired a shot close to the head of another brave woman who dared to withstand them. They even attacked and threw stones at an old woman aged eighty-two years. At Cranberry Breaker, they halted while a detachment went to Crystal Ridge for reinforcements, repeating there the outrages of Harwood and Cranberry. Those who remained further armed themselves from a heap of scrap iron near the breaker. The mob consisted of men from Humboldt, Harwood, Cranberry and Crystal Ridge, and proceeded on their riotous march, shouting, cursing, and firing on those on those who sought to escape. At West Hazleton strippings, they drove the men from work and then proceeded to enter the borough.

"Here they were overtaken by the sheriff followed by his posse. He struck their column well to the rear. He ordered them to halt. They refused. One man shouted, 'No stop, s— of a b————.' As they swept him along, he read his proclamation to them as best he could, then ploughed his way through the surging mass to the head of their line. Here, the deputies, having hurried forward, took position along a fence and partly across the street, covering the sheriff with their guns. He demanded to know where they were going. They yelled in reply, 'To Lattimer, to stop the works!' The sheriff then read his proclamation a second time, told them who he was, and commanded, begged and implored them to keep the peace. They only became the more violent, shouting, cursing, and gesticulating, threatening the sheriff and dashing toward him with stones in their hands while he strove to hold them back by menacing them with a drawn revolver.

The tumult so increased that some of the deputies came to his aid and also urged the rioters to disperse. They refused, shouting, 'We go to Lattimer to stop the mine.' The sheriff plainly told them they would not be allowed to do that, or if they did, they would have to kill him first. They became so turbulent that bystanders were warned to go to their homes, as shooting was likely to occur. The mob threw stones at the deputies, who clubbed them back with the butts of their guns. One raised a rock above his head in both hands, with the apparent intent of hurling it at deputy Platt. Instantly, guns were leveled at him and he dropped the rock. The rioters taunted and jeered at the deputies, 'Go to hell,' they yelled; 'you aren't soldiers, you can't stop us; shoot, you s—— of b——, shoot you dare no shoot.' The same man shouted, 'We're going to Lattimer to raise hell.' This sentiment seemed to meet the approval of the mob, for another took up the cry and yelled, 'We go to Lattimer to raise hell.' Another shouted out the threat, 'Tomorrow we'll all bring guns and you'll see whether you'll stop us then.'

"The result of this encounter was that the mob drew off into a field by the side of the road, where a man who stood under a tree made a speech to them in some foreign tongue. The sheriff and his posse then withdrew up the street in the hope that the mob, seeing the determined stand taken by the authorities, would give up their desperate project.

"Soon, however, word was received that they had reorganized and were marching to Lattimer by another road, which passed around West Hazleton.

"The sheriff and his men then hurriedly boarded a trolley car that ran back into Hazleton and out by the Lattimer line as far as Harleigh. Here they left their car and took position on a hillside to see whether the mob still intended to proceed to Lattimer. When the rioters saw the deputies and their car, they withdrew to one side of the road and appeared to be in consultation. Presently, they resumed their march and took the Lattimer road. The sheriff and his men re-entered their car and ran around and ahead of the marching crowd to Farley's Hotel. There they were joined by the deputies stationed at Lattimer, some of the men finding room in the regular car which immediately followed. On this car were some other passengers, among them Welch, Yeager and a person known as the 'big Hungarian,' of whom you will hear more presently. In the meantime, swift riders on bicycles had carried the news of the mob's advance to Lattimer. The people were terrified—sent to the school for their children and fled from their homes in every direction save that from which the mob was advancing.

"The trolley car again ran around and ahead of the mob. At the entrance to Lattimer village, the deputies left the cars as did also some others, including Welch, Yeager and the 'big Hungarian.' The deputies lined up along the fence in front of the first house on the left as you go into Lattimer— the left of the line extending across and a short distance beyond the entrance to an alley between the first house and the second, while the right of the line extended further than the end of the fence in front of the house.

"We shall show you that when the rush came, the mob spread out to cover the entire front of the deputies' line and leaving the road swept over this intervening space, where men were killed within fifteen feet of the line of deputies, having charged straight at them over more than seventy feet after they had left the Lattimer road.

"The deputies being lined up as I have stated, the sheriff told them to keep cool and said that he would go forward and meet the mob, and make another effort to induce them to disperse and keep the peace.

"He ordered them to halt, which some in the front ranks did for a moment, those behind closing up, some crowding upon him while others pushed by and closed in behind. He asked them where they were going and for what purpose. Several voices shouted back, 'We go to Lattimer to stop the mines.' He told them, as he had at West Hazleton, that they

65

should not do this but should disperse and keep the peace. He then tried to read his proclamation, but the mob was in no mood for talk. Several shouted, 'Go on, go on,' while one guy who was near the sheriff called out, 'Go ahead, him son of bitch, him no good. We go to Lattimer to stop the mines.' The sheriff reached forward and grasped this man to place him under arrest. Instantly there was a tumult of yells. Five or six men pounced upon the sheriff, seized him, shoved him into a ditch on the left of the road and began beating him, two of them flourished revolvers at him and a third made a savage stab at him with a knife. The sheriff, in his struggles freed his right arm and drew his revolver and snapped it at one of his assistants. It would not go off. Instantly, the man, Nevatna, struck him a vicious blow in the face with his fist and knocked him to his knees. He would have fallen flat, but for the crowd surrounding him, many of them with their backs to the deputies. In the meantime, the main body of the mob was rushing down upon the little band of eighty deputies. All at once, a revolver shot rang out from the rushing mob, then another, then three close together, then a rattling volley from the guns, which lasted a few seconds, less than half a minute, and ceased when the mob gave way.

"How did the firing begin? We shall show you, gentlemen.

"As the deputies lined up, Welch, Yeager and the 'big Hungarian' and some others stationed themselves at the entrance to the alley in the rear of the line. When the sheriff advanced to meet the mob and while he was talking to them, Welch, Yeager and the Hungarian, who were in their shirt sleeves, raised their arms and beckoned to the mob to come on—and they did come, with howls and yells, that mass of furious men came rushing down the road, away from the road, across the intervening ground, straight at the line of deputies. Then from the charging men a shot was fired, then another, then the big Hungarian in the alley in the rear fired three shots in quick succession from a revolver, one of them

66

point-blank at Deputy Price, who avoided the shot by dropping to his knees. The Hungarian then dashed through the line of deputies to join his friends in front and fell in the rattling volley that followed. The order to fire was given by whom we do not know, but it was none too soon, for the head of the charging column had rushed within fifteen feet of the deputies' line. Many of the men were killed and wounded, while Deputy Treible was shot through both arms by some person in the rear of the deputies. When the rioters had fled, the sheriff and his posse proceeded to care for the wounded and dying. With all possible humanity and tenderness, they gave them such as they could. That, gentlemen, is the story of Lattimer as you will hear it from the defendant's witnesses and when you have heard it, and have listened to the charge of the Court upon the law of the case, we shall hope acquittal, a verdict that will say to the world that these men did no deed of crime, but did their duty as faithful officers and as defenders of that liberty under law which we have received from our fathers and, please God, shall yet hand down to our children."

The defense, in a patriotic appeal, went on to say:

" 'But,' says counsel, 'they carried the American flag, and these deputies did not respect the flag. They tore the flag and fired on the men that carried it.'

"Was there ever such an appeal to patriotism before! A band of unnaturalized foreigners assembled to prevent American citizens from exercising their right to labor, head their procession with the Stars and Stripes, and endeavor to give a lawful character to their unlawful acts by shielding themselves under the flag. Probably they ignorantly believed that no one would dare fire on the flag.

"As well and reasonably might Confederate soldiers have raised the Stars and Stripes and claimed immunity for their rebellious attempts to destroy the government.

"The glorious flag of the republic, now known and honored throughout the earth, with not a single stripe erased or

67

polluted and not a single star obscured, preserved in its integrity and beauty by a sacrifice that brought tears and sorrow to every home in the land, was desecrated when carried by a tumultuous mob bent on breaking and defying the law."

The sheriff's posse was acquitted.

The Court proceedings brought forth a barrage of editorial comment from eastern newspapers. A sampling of the editorial reaction reflects the division in national thought. From a sampling it appears that the voices of law and order were louder than those sympathetic to the dead.

The *New York Sun* said: "The acquittal of Sheriff Martin and his deputies on the charge of murder, because of their armed resistance to the mob at Lattimer, is a victory for law and order. Every effort at the intimidation of judge and jury was made by incendiary journalism, but the trial proceeded fairly and evenly to its conclusion in the verdict rendered yesterday in strict accordance with the evidence. The result proves that American civilization is safe under the protection of the law."

Many newspapers found the verdict unfair, even appalling. Several samples of these opinions are quoted here.

The *New York Evening Journal* editorialized: "To the jury who brought in the verdict, in the face of evidence overwhelming; to the judge whose charge and general conduct have been as free from the judicial quality as the howling hyena, the *Evening Journal* extends the assurance of its most profound contempt."

The *Scranton Times* editorial read: "Though legally declared innocent, however, Sheriff Martin and his deputies cannot evade the moral guilt of the shedding of human blood. If the interpretation of the law as to the powers of the sheriff in time of strike, made by Judge Woodward in his charge, is correct, and we presume it is, then the sheriff is an absolute autocrat. The least disturbance authorizes him to call out the power of the county and legalizes any act, no matter how brutal and atrocious, that may be perpetrated by the posse.

"The sheriff's posse of today is an irresponsible body. It is not controlled by the sheriff and it lacks self-control. It is not in harmony with the age we live in, and it ought to be abolished for some more civilized method of keeping the peace. This is one of the lessons of the Lattimer trial, and it is a lesson that ought to be acted upon at the very next session of the Pennsylvania Legislature."

The *Hazleton Standard*, looking toward new indictments (which never came) was still distressed. "The verdict in the trial of Sheriff Martin and his deputies is what was expected by everybody who followed the proceedings since the case began. As was plainly evident, the demonstrations that the metropolitan journals have been predicting did not take place when the verdict became public property. It is only fair to presume that the jury did as the law would have them do— be governed by and render their decision according to the evidence as they saw it. In this the sheriff and his men had the advantage, because no witness for the Commonwealth proved that any one of the defendants fired the fatal shots, yet the fact remains that but one deputy would admit of firing even one bullet. The deputies did the best swearing, and as a consequence, are liberated in the eyes of the law from the charge of taking the lives of Mike Ceslak and his companions."

The *Elmira Gazette* editorialized: "The verdict is not surprising. This result was predicted from the beginning of the prosecution. The jury ostensibly bases its decision on the grounds that the disturbance of the peace and the danger to the sheriff and his posse were such that the shooting was justifiable. The actual reason, however, is probably the impression that conviction would lessen the vigor of officers of the law when new turmoils shall arise and inspire weak and cowardly opposition to future creators of disorder. The view that public policy required support of the sheriff and his deputies, even though they had done more than was necessary, was in reality the main prop of the defense. No reasonable doubt exists that the dispersion of the body of marchers did not require the killing of eighteen [sic] and the wounding of forty. A half dozen shots, if shots were necessary, would have done as well as the fusillades which caused this fearful slaughter. The deputies yielded to the frenzy of the moment. The jury, in reaching the decision chronicled, must have been swayed by the sense that, on a debatable issue between the mob and the sheriff, the verdict must incline toward the representatives of the law."

Still, the Lattimer killings influenced the life of the people in the anthracite region more than was perceived at the time. In the whirling melting-pot of the mining-industrial communities, the visibility of the "newer nationalities" began to replace the suspicions and antagonisms of "hunkies," "polaks," and "dagoes." The transition was not dramatic nor immediate, but the experiences of the Lattimer event and trial permeated the sensitive consciousness of many, so that the disdainful segregation of the mine-patch began to disintegrate.

The trial with its decision seemed to prove that, as through the ages, justice is taught by stark injustice. The verdict, seen as an injustice to the miners, brought new empathic identification. The right to protect their interests and the right to organize were strongly enhanced.

Five years later when young John Mitchell appeared in the region, the Lattimer tragedy still represented exploitation and injustice. While the defense of the coal company had tried to picture the miners as violent anarchists in the tradition of the Molly Maguires, the community did not accept this analogy. The verdict, not guilty for the posse, was not evidence that the community feared miners so much as it was a reluctant disposition to find their prestigious neighbors guilty of murder.

Out of Lattimer there emerged a somewhat increased respect for ethnic groups, and a partial recognition of injustices among anthracite miners. Throughout the whole Hazleton area especially, there was a cry for a more merciful law and order and community peace.

Today Lattimer Mines still stands, a stone's throw off Route 309 on the southern border of Hazleton. More than a dozen company houses remain, their exteriors covered with fresh paint or aluminum siding, brighter than they were in 1897. However, even the few new ranch-style homes built along the main street have not perceptibly changed the little settlement. The only visible reminder of the Lattimer Massacre is a granite marker erected by the United Council of Luzerne and Carbon Counties, both A. F. of L. and C. I. O. The inscription reads:

> It was not a battle because they were not aggressive, nor were they on the defensive because they had no weapons of any kind and were simply shot down like so many worthless objects; Each of the life-takers trying to out-do the others in the butchering.

On September 10, an unseasonably hot day, 400 mine workers marched from Harwood to Lattimer, the last collierey working in the Hazleton area during the severe general strike there in 1897.

Many of the marching mine workers escaped the gunfire by crawling through this culvert.

CHAPTER VI

Overcoming Ethnic Differences
to Build a Union

John Mitchell and the United Mine Workers

In the nearly one hundred year history of Pennsylvania An-thracite, John Mitchell is by far the most popular and revered leader among miners. He was not a native Pennsylvanian. In Braidwood, Illinois, where John Mitchell was born in 1870, the breaker was called a tipple and dominated the landscape there as did the breaker in Avondale. In Braid-wood, the company store exploited the mine workers as it did in Northeastern Pennsylvania.

From Braidwood, Mitchell learned about surviving on wages of $400 a year. But, most of all, when he went to work in the mines at Braidwood at thirteen years of age, he observed and learned the life habits of a miner; the boy learned of the loneliness, the shooting, blasting, the timbering, track-laying, and the preparation for actual mining, the "dead work," for which there was no pay or recompense from the company.

As a boy of thirteen, he knew the cage ride, the drop of 1,000 feet or more into near total blackness, with only a wick oil lamp on his cap. He started as a trapper-boy or a "patcher." He moved up the mining hierarchy, as did the mining chil-dren of Pennsylvania, from patcher to mule driver to miner's helper and finally, to company miner or even contract miner.

At Braidwood, too, he experienced the suspicions and prejudices of ethnic groups. The pattern of influx was the same there as in the East: first, the English, Welsh and Irish, then the Italians and the Slavs, including Polish, Lithuanian, Russian and Slovak. In Braidwood, he heard and knew the disdain, the hurt and occasionally the humor in "Greenhorn," "Cheese-eater," "Hunky," "Polack," "Dago," or "Harp."

The father of John Mitchell was Scotch-Irish, an Orangeman who married three times. John Mitchell was a son by the second marriage. Of the mother of Mitchell, Martha Halley, little is known. When Mitchell's father was killed by a runaway team of horses, four sets of children were housed with Mitchell's stepmother in extreme poverty. Mitchell, as a child, appears to have been humiliated and shamed by his school absences due to his chores at home, washing clothes, weeding the garden, and doing much of the housework for the widowed family. He left the family household at ten years of age to work on a farm for his keep and one dollar a week. When he was thirteen, he returned to Braidwood to work in the mines. He became a trapper, called patcher in the anthracite region, running to open and close ventilating doors in the mines for the mule drivers and their trip of cars.

When he was sixteen, with years of experience in the mines, he went west, maturing as he rode the rails, bumming, finding jobs in the mines of Colorado, New Mexico, and Wyoming. The boy became a man. Slight of build, weighing 120 pounds, he was wiry and strong and returned to Braidwood dedicated to justice through organization. Much later, as he gained weight and matured physically, he was a rather striking figure with his dark hair and coloring, and since he had acquired the habit of wearing the long black professional-looking garb of the day, he was often mistaken for a priest. Thousands of miners during the years thought of him as a "good Catholic," even though he was, in reality, reared a Presbyterian and only later converted to Catholicism.

As a young teenager, John Mitchell stood and took the oath of the Knights of Labor, saying in part: "We mean no conflict with necessary enterprise, no antagonism to necessary capital." The oath taken in the mining camp of Braidwood was to touch and inflame the anthracite towns of Pennsylvania. For the rest of his life, John Mitchell would keep that oath in his heart and mind. But he couldn't forestall the conflicts and antagonisms. They were inherent in the injustices of mining, injustices as apparent in the mining camps of Illinois, Ohio, Colorado, and West Virginia as they were in the boroughs of Pennsylvania.

When John Mitchell was twenty, District No. 135 of the Knights of Labor joined with the National Progressive Union in Columbus, Ohio, on January 22, 1890, to create the United Mine Workers of America. The mine workers, despite the ambitious title, were far from united, and covered very little of America. However, it was a time for presumption, for the workers of the nation were restless. Populists, Coxey's Army, and railroad workers were all on the march. The oratory of William Jennings Bryan was more powerful than his platform, but it helped to sensitize America to the plight of labor.

During the time of rising aspirations for American labor, William D. Ryan, a union official, brought John Mitchell into the officialdom of labor. Ryan saw in Mitchell qualities of conviction, self-sacrifice, and thoughtfulness. Others also saw these qualities, and Mitchell was elected secretary-treasurer of a district of the union in Illinois. He was soon promoted and became a lobbyist for the miners at the state capital in Springfield.

Today, as one stands near the courthouse in Scranton's central city and looks at the statue of John Mitchell, one presumes that he must have been a typical rabble-rousing orator of the Gilded Age. He was not. Mitchell was thoughtful, conversational, organized. He was generally the last to speak and had the ability to synthesize and summarize. Addressing the miners, he spoke with authority. Their needs,

75

their injustices, their suffering had been his. He did not need to shout. In conference with operators or officials, he was temperate, knowledgeable, and compromising.

Mitchell's manner made him suspect by the impatient and extremists; however, it made him acceptable to organizations like the National Civic Foundation, dedicated to reform, labor peace, and justice through the joint action of labor, capital and government.

Too, John Mitchell was attacked not only by more radical reformers than he, but also by those who cast doubts about his many business enterprises. An article published in *Labor History*, "The Acquisitive Spirit of John Mitchell" by James O. Monroe, looks back at Mitchell's stock market investments and personal business interests. Monroe faults Mitchell for investments seeming to exploit Mitchell's closeness to labor and to coal. However, the rank and file of his union, laborers, breaker boys, miners were not influenced by these charges, most of which emerged after the 1902 strike. To mine workers, Mitchell was the uncontaminated leader despite the criticism of Mother Jones and others.

When John Mitchell began his national career in the United Mine Workers, the industries of steel, mining, railroading, building, and manufacturing created a great number of millionaires. Their conspicuous spending of new wealth created a new name in the United States' vocabulary. The Gilded Age had arrived. The magnificent mansions on Fifth Avenue competed with each other in extravagances. Newport was the summer playground of the wealthy, the "playground of plunderers." The ballroom of the Waldorf, prepared for a ball in 1897, was decorated as the palace at Versailles, and one guest from a wealthy family wore a gold-plated suit of armor designed at a cost of $10,000. Very little of this wealth trickled down to labor. The wealth was seemingly beyond the reach of the unorganized and sometimes disorganized workers. It was in the environment of the Gilded Age in

1897, that John Mitchell, at twenty-seven years of age, was baptized as a leader in a major labor dispute.

The strike of 1897 began on July 4 with patriotic parades. It came at a time when the operators least expected it and they had no time to build up the coal reserves as they had in the past. The strike started in northern Illinois but the other districts were slow to respond. Mitchell's assignment was to organize southern Illinois. Known as "Little Egypt,[1]" it was tough territory. The usual problems of organizing were worsened by elements of Kentucky feuding and the importation of blacks, who suffered from the skepticism and prejudices of the area. Eventually over 100,000 miners struck in one of the first massive movements in labor history. With the support of Eugene Debs, Mother Jones, W. D. Mahon of the Streetcar Union, James O'Connell of the Machinists Union, the American Federation of Labor, and the remnants of the Knights of Labor, the miners won their first victory.

Following the victory, John Mitchell went to his first national convention at Columbus, Ohio. It was there that he saw the delegates in their long coats and wide hats and bought a similar outfit for himself, the style identifying him for years to come. At the convention, he witnessed the heated antagonism of labor politics, the competition for high office and leadership. He learned that any victory was always subject to the slings and arrows of the cry of disdain: "sellout."

When Mitchell got home to Spring Valley, where he lived with his wife and children, he was greeted with praise and parades. He was a national organizer, but in Braidwood, he was a hero. The miners of Spring Valley had achieved one of their great objectives, the eight-hour day for bituminous miners (though not for anthracite miners), and they were proud of their neighbor for bringing it home. For Mitchell,

---

[1] The area between the Ohio and Mississippi rivers resembled the Nile Delta. This section of Illinois was known as Little Egypt.

it was a great day. The old days of picking, hammering, shoveling, crouching, dynamiting, and coughing were over. But it also meant a life separated from family and children. Mitchell had married Catherine O'Rourke when he was twenty-two and she was twenty-four. They had six children, two of whom had died in infancy.

Mitchell's next organizational challenge was in West Virginia. Today a stronghold of the United Mine Workers, it was then one of the least organized states. Mitchell's efforts there were unsuccessful. After two years, there were only three hundred and seventy-five U.M.W.A. members in West Virginia. Because of his lack of success, Mitchell was transferred from West Virginia to the more familiar territory in southern Illinois where he was more successful.

At a meeting of the National Executive Board, called in 1899 to receive the resignation of President Ratchford, Mitchell was named acting president. At the same time the board called for an election in 1899. Mitchell was considered by many to be too young to be elected president, especially against experienced U.M.W.A. in-fighters such as W. T. Lewis and T. L. Lewis, brothers from Ohio, and Pat Dolan of Pennsylvania. Nevertheless, Mitchell did run and was elected president by an overwhelming vote.

Mitchell revealed executive ability, and like all great executives in industry and labor, he was supported by an extremely capable executive secretary, Elizabeth Catherine Morris. She not only organized his records, but edited and corrected the grammar of his speeches. Morris served him for twenty years, remembering faces, plans, details, and promises to keep. She was invaluable to the "boy president" of 1900 as he stood on the threshold of the anthracite challenge, from where he propelled himself into national recognition.

In 1900, when Mitchell turned his eyes toward the great hard-coal region of Pennsylvania, the remnants of the Knights of Labor and the Workers' Benevolent Association were still

78

intact. In addition, a few U.M.W.A. locals were functioning. Mitchell focused his attention and efforts on the anthracite area because Ben James, one of the three delegates from the region to the 1899 convention, had requested the organization of the anthracite fields. Until then the coal operators had always played the anthracite and bituminous workers against each other. Mitchell's main argument, designed to win approval of the James resolution, was that the availability of anthracite should not be used by the operators to defeat the bituminous coal miners. Ben James knew, too, that union leaders could not delay a real anthracite push. Conditions were intolerable: anthracite dockages, deductions taken from the pay of miners for rock and other impurities found in the coal were more unjust, costs of supplies exorbitant, hours longer, child labor more cruelly widespread, and death and accident tolls higher than in the worst period of soft-coal history.

John Mitchell moved into the anthracite with some concern. He remembered his failure in West Virginia. He remembered the conflicts and ethnic rivalries. The successive waves of English, Welsh, and Irish followed by the Italians and Slavs were a major obstruction to unity and John Mitchell knew it. The hatred and bitterness between the groups came from the "recollection that these foreigners . . . had been imported as strikebreakers by the thousands between 1875 and 1887." The prejudices were based on misinformation and exaggerated distortions, yet they existed, and that worried Mitchell.

Mitchell embarked on his mission in the anthracite region and spoke in halls, in fields, and in homes. Using his deliberate reasoning and his direct speech, he brought a new enthusiasm into the area. Without oratory, he met the ethnic problem head-on, saying, "The coal you dig isn't Slavish, Polish, or Irish coal, it's coal." He pleaded for the end of the terms, "hunky," "dago," and all the other expletives. Knowing the influence of the church, and perhaps remem-

79

bering the misunderstandings between Terence Powderly and the religious hierarchy, he visited as many of the clergy as he could, always pleading his cause. He was successful. Bishop Hoban, from the archdiocese of the Wilkes-Barre/Scranton area, Father J. J. Curran, of Wilkes-Barre, and Father Phillips, of Hazleton, became strong supporters.

Mitchell courted business as well. Through John J. Loftus, a Scranton pharmacist, he convinced segments of the business community that higher wages produced greater purchasing power and, therefore, higher profits for merchants.

Perhaps the largest obstacle to the struggle for organization was the control of the anthracite fields by the railroads of the Morgan and Vanderbilt interests. In the early years of anthracite mining, independent operators owned the mines. But as the production and markets for "black diamonds" increased, the owners of the monopolistic railroads moved in to control the production and marketing of anthracite.

Although Mitchell organized for five months, the number of memberships numbered only 10,000 out of a work force of 150,000. Mitchell knew it was a start, but he was prepared to make his first demands from the anthracite mine operators. The year was 1900. The time was right. The anthracite workers had not had a wage increase since 1880. The miners demanded higher wages, a decrease in the price of blasting powder, relief from the arbitrary docking of wages for coal deemed unfit for sale, (operators refused to pay for loaded cars which they claimed had too much rock) and a uniform standard of 2240 pounds (instead of the long ton of 2400 pounds) for a loaded car of coal.[2]

Mitchell was unsure of the local and national reaction to the strike demands. He especially feared the reaction from consumers in New York, Philadelphia, Boston and other areas using anthracite. Too, it was easy to rally the miners

---

[2] Long ton was 2400 pounds. Short ton was 2000 pounds. Coal was weighed at the mines by the long ton. When sold to consumers, the short ton was used.

against the absentee owners, Morgan and Vanderbilt,[3] but against a local owner like John Markle, a reasonable man, it was difficult. Markle had even offered to arbitrate. Mitchell puzzled. Should he negotiate separately with Markle, breaking the united front of Northeastern Pennsylvania, and try for a piecemeal settlement. He chose a unified attack. He converted Father Phillips to his position, and the Hazleton men remained loyal and struck.

The miners and Mitchell received additional help from a strange source, a stereotyped capitalist and coal operator, Mark Hanna. Hanna, managing the "full dinner pail" campaign of William McKinley, wanted labor's support. Actually Hanna may have been a more complex man than his caricatures portrayed him. He seemed to have an interest in working men, was a leader in the National Civic Foundation, a non-partisan reform organization, and was an industrialist who feared financiers and bankers. Even if he saw labor unions only as a necessary evil, he did recognize them as part of an emerging, complex new democracy.

When the strike of 1900 began, Mitchell told the miner's story so convincingly that the *New York Times* proclaimed their cause a just one. Even more importantly, Mitchell told the miner's story so precisely and honestly that he cemented feelings, not only of all the miners, but of their wives and families as well. Moving through the anthracite communities, this priestly-appearing figure inspired support unmatched in coal history. One wife is said to have kept her husband's mining clothes in her washer, lest he return to the mines as a scab.

Victory came when Mark Hanna went over the heads of the operators, directly to J. P. Morgan and arranged a meeting between Morgan and Mitchell. Very soon after that meet-

---

[3] The financial institution of J. P. Morgan and Cornelius Vanderbilt, owners of a network of railroads, controlled the shipment of anthracite and continued to acquire more and more coal producing companies. By 1923, the railroads owned 80 per cent of the mined coal and 90 per cent of future reserves.

ing, the other operators and railroad presidents, who were mine owners, received orders from the Hanna and Morgan banking, railroad, and mining trusts to negotiate and settle.

The settlement of the strike of 1900 was a real victory for the miners. They won a ten percent increase in wages, recognition by the owners of miners' grievance committees, and relief from excessive charges for powder, charges which were reduced by one hundred percent. The new contract, to expire in April, 1901, although not providing for the union recognition that Mitchell wanted, expressed the need for a grievance procedure. The contract ended the chaotic feudalism of anthracite mining. The day the strike was settled, October 29, became a holiday for the industry, and "me Johnny Mitchell man," became a favorite phrase, especially with his followers among the Slavs and Italians. Mitchell's popularity was so great that when news of the President's assassination circulated, many of these miners believed Mitchell had been shot. President to them meant John Mitchell, not William McKinley. Mitchell was hailed as a Moses, a Lincoln, a Savior. He accepted a gold medal bought by contributions from twenty thousand breaker boys. He reciprocated. Mitchell turned over much of his twelve hundred dollar annual salary to a memorial for the victims of the Lattimer Massacre which had taken place four years earlier on September 10, 1897. At the height of his popularity, Mitchell might well have considered his anthracite efforts with 150,000 organized miners a success.

But three goals were unachieved. The anthracite miners still were bound to a nine-hour day, one hour longer than bituminous workers; the weighing system was still unfair to miners; and the grievance procedure machinery was not complete. John Mitchell felt these objectives could be achieved. In 1902, he decided to go after them. When he did, he initiated a chain of events which resulted in the largest and most publicized strike in American labor history to that date.

Mitchell's chief obstacle in the memorable labor struggle was George F. Baer of the Philadelphia and Reading Railroad. The Reading Railroad controlled fifty percent of the production of all anthracite. The older George F. Baer was a formidable opponent for the youthful John Mitchell, now thirty-two years old. The dispute was a colorful conflict between the powerful lawyer, Baer, and the young, capable, single-minded, justice-seeking Mitchell.

As the strike drew near, Mitchell had to hold the miners in check. Remembering their gains of 1901, the miners were restless, aggressive and over-demanding. Mitchell, more realistic, hoped to win the respect and cooperation of the operators by convincing them of the futility of a strike. He suggested a new contract with a ten percent increase, but was willing to concede a continuation of the nine-hour day. The operators misinterpreted this reasonableness as weakness. Nevertheless, Mitchell kept the miners working four weeks beyond the expiration of the old contract in the hope of averting a walkout. It was to no avail. On May 12, 1902, Mitchell ordered the men, nearly 150,000 out of the mines. Even then, John W. "Bet a Million" Gates, an odds-maker, offered 100 to 1 against a strike. When the delegates of the miners voted it was 461½ for and 394¾ against the strike. And so the strike, considered by many historians to be the most important in American labor history, began. It eventually created an energy shortage matched only by the oil crisis of the 1970's.

It is interesting to note the wages of mining men as the strike started. While the term miners is used generally to denote those employed in the mines, it should be remembered that the miner specifically was the employee charged with directing and blasting coal from the seams. His aide was a miner's helper or laborer. A miner received about one dollar a car or about six dollars a day. He paid for his own powder and also paid his helper, who received two dollars a day. The miner usually earned sixty dollars to one hundred dollars a month, the helper forty a month if he worked full time. Breaker boys earned seventy-five cents a day.

From the beginning, the operators sensed an early victory, based not on issues, but on the expectation that the membership, disappointed in the conservatism of Mitchell, would drop him for a more radical leader. The operators felt that a more radical leader would alienate the public and destroy the union completely. Too, as always, the miners were expected to give up when they ran out of money.

Mitchell, who would have preferred compromise, found himself in a position of conflict. As leader, he first had to control the miners to prevent another Lattimer Massacre or Haymarket.[4] Then, to insure public support, he befriended sociologists, humanitarians, and writers. John R. Commons, a labor historian, Walter Weyl, founder of *The New Republic*, John Graham Brooks, and Harry Lloyd, all became spokesmen for the cause. Mitchell also won support from a great segment of the press. In Washington, the administration appeared to be sympathetic. Mitchell seemed to have support previously denied to him. Still, corporate power and its voices were far from overwhelmed. The battle for public opinion was on. As in many battles, victory came not from numbers or strategy, but from a mistake. The circumstances were these:

A Wilkes-Barre photographer, William F. Clark, saw the strike strangling the American economy and its people. He wrote the following letter to the president of the Philadelphia and Reading Railroad Company, George F. Baer, the spokesman for the coal operators:

---

[4] Haymarket. A square in Chicago. There on May 4, 1886, radical leaders organized a rally to protest police brutality against striking factory workers. Police tried to disband the meeting. A bomb exploded killing eight policemen and two others.

Mr. Baer, President of the Philadelphia and Reading Railroad Company,

Dear Sir:

With all respect, I beg to address you with reference to the present coal strike. I note again your absolute refusal to do anything further to bring about a satisfactory adjustment of the great labor difficulty. From the beginning, I have followed it up with interest and have noted the refusal to consider the interest of miner or public at large. I believe you to be a man of good judgment and that you no doubt have given this matter great consideration in your own way, but, as you remarked, it was not a religious matter. I believe it possible for man to err unless we do things at all times in God's way. While it is true it is not a religious matter, yet it is possible to take Christ in all our business affairs and by so doing we have nothing to lose, but all to gain. Man in himself, in his weakness and frailty, is not always capable of using the best judgment. There is no doubt that both sides feel oppressed, but if operators would take Christ in their business and labor unions would take Christ in their unions, this oppression would soon disappear and each would consider the other a brother, for indeed such we are in Christ Jesus; I pray God will hasten the day when this may be—when we shall be willing to listen to each other, if not individually, then through organizations of God-fearing, God-loving men. We all know the horrors of the mine, the dangers seen and unseen and may see the ambulance going from mine to hospital daily. We go back only a few days to recall the awful horror at Johnstown,[5] and it makes our hearts ring with pain and pity for widows and fatherless children, who mourn and cannot be comforted, only in the hope that lies in Christ Jesus. Can we altogether ignore their appeal?

Is there not a way to appease all sides? Must all be crushed because a few are unreasonable? Can we not recall the mercy God was willing to show Sodom and Gomorrah if ten righteous persons could be found and deal with these men ac-

---

[5] The reference is to the Johnstown Flood of 1889. The Connemaugh Dam owned by a sportsman's club, collapsed and flooded the city of Johnstown, Pennsylvania, drowning 2000 citizens.

cordingly? Will you not reason again what would Christ do in my stead, or will you hold in your hand the lever of industry and persistently say, I will not relax, notwithstanding that mighty empires have fallen which cared not for man and neither regarded God? It is not possible to bring about an adjustment of peace and good will in some way by granting an increase, however small, on condition of a three or five year contract, with the idea that all petty strikes shall be averted and the union notify the men through Mr. Mitchell that the organization will not stand by any man who disregards orders or attempts to precipitate trouble not justifiable to a board of arbitration, that all bosses be notified not to be partial or receive money for best places? Under these conditions, I believe all would gladly return to work and you would have the respect of the nation and the blessing of God.

I believe it worth giving it another trial, as the men feel that the last increase was easily gotten back through the increase in the price of coal. With the operator lies the power without consulting the consumer. Thus why should thousands be crushed and go down to satisfy one desire? I pray God to send the Holy Spirit to reason in your heart and to act accordingly and be the means of lifting thousands to a better way of living and finally to purer, nobler lives.

My father came from Scotland when a boy and early in manhood entered the mines, where he spent the best part of his life. It was a great struggle for him and my dear mother, now gone to her eternal reward, to provide for their family, which by the grace of God they did with the determination that the boys should not face the dangers of the mine, which when a boy I often heard him speak about, and recall my anxious mother until his safe return home again. Those were anxious days for all, but sunshine came at last and my father was able to better his position outside of the mines, never to return again.

It is with these recollections my heart goes out in pity for the toilers of the mine and I do not pass one with his blackened face and tired tread but that I say, God pity him, and I again appeal—consider them once more for the sake of Him who suffered and died on Calvary to save us all. Yours sincerely,

Wm. F. Clark

86

The reply of George F. Baer became a landmark in American labor history, an egregious error and was widely reproduced to illustrate his arrogance. Union leaders published it often to reveal what they saw as the attitude of all captains of industry. Labor historians have quoted it interminably as a landmark anti-labor statement. Baer replied.

Philadelphia and Reading Railway Company, President's Office, Reading Terminal

Philadelphia, July 17, 1902

Mr. W. F. Clark, Wilkes-Barre, Pennsylvania

My dear Mr. Clark:

I have your letter of the 16th instant.

I do not know who you are. I see that you are a religious man; but you are evidently biased in favor of the right of the working man to control a business in which he has no other interest than to secure fair wages for the work he does.

I beg of you not be discouraged. The rights and interests of the laboring man will be protected and cared for—not only by the labor agitators, but by the Christian men to whom God in His infinite wisdom has given the control of the property interests of the country, and upon the successful management of which so much depends.

Do not be discouraged. Pray earnestly that right may triumph, always remembering that the Lord God Omnipotent still reigns, and that His reign is one of law and order, and not violence and crime. Yours truly,

George F. Baer, President

The line, . . . "by Christian men to whom God in His infinite wisdom has given the control of the property interest of the country." provoked a barrage of letters and editorials from a broad spectrum of writers and clergymen.

The presumption in Baer's letter self-righteously identifying God with the operators was infuriating to the miners. The audacity which leaked through Baer's pietism was shocking, not only to labor, but to much of the public as well. But

87

even the public outrage against Baer's letter was not enough to move the operators to the settlement table.

The coal crises of 1901 and 1902 strangled the economy. Railroads curtailed services, factories shut down, schools closed, hospitals were threatened. The atmosphere in the towns became tense. Merchants strained under credit demands. Citizens resented the soldiers walking the streets to keep peace. Girls insulted the soldiers. Miners said bayonets could not mine a single ton of coal. Meanwhile, coal shortages and the strike made headlines every day. In Chicago, people seeking fuel were apprehended picking the wooden paving blocks from the streets. New York Democrats called for the nationalization of the industry.

Out of this tense environment came the call of President Theodore Roosevelt for a White House meeting of all parties. The two antagonists, John Mitchell and George Baer, met face to face. With Mitchell were two officers of the union, John Fahy and Thomas Duffy. With Baer were W. H. Truesdale, David Wilson and John Markle, representing the independent operators. President Roosevelt, aware of his lack of authority, invoked patriotism and pleaded for peace. Mitchell, the first to speak, was conciliatory and offered to accept any decision of a presidential commission. The operators did not reply, but requested a temporary adjournment for consideration. When the group reconvened, the operators replied with a torrent of inflammatory words about law and order. Mr. Baer lectured the president and implored him "not to waste time with fomenters of anarchy . . . but to do what was done in the war of rebellion—restore the majesty of the law." He spoke of the miners as the forces of violence with Mitchell as chief." In an interview, Baer was quoted as saying of miners, "They don't suffer; why, they can't even speak English."

The inconclusive meeting prompted a volley of extreme editorial solutions, including government intervention and even military invasion. Fortunately, none of these recommendations was accepted. It was rumored that Roosevelt was dismayed by the attitude of the participants, confiding to some that Mitchell was the only "gentleman" in the group. The president gave the strike priority over other national matters. Seeing Mitchell as the most reasonable of the group, Roosevelt asked him to send the miners back to work while he appointed a board of conciliation to work out a solution. Mitchell knew that the operators would not accept these recommendations, as they had not done in the past, therefore, he refused conciliation, that is compromise arranged by a third party and agreed upon by both sides. He asked instead for arbitration, a technique which would compel operators to accept any dictated solution.

Roosevelt's autobiography reveals that when Mitchell refused conciliation, he considered a plan to have the governor of Pennsylvania send in troops. Under the plan, the governor was to request the President to keep the peace. Then, the army would displace the operators but would also protect any miner desiring to work. However, before any specific plan of action could be imposed, word came that the operators would accept arbitration. Mitchell accepted the arbitration offer, but immediately was accused by Mother Jones, Benjamin Packard of the British Miners Federation, and other labor leaders of "selling out." But a convention of the miners in the three anthracite districts ratified Mitchell's decision. Mitchell proclaimed, "These poor, underpaid . . . have . . . taught these corporate managers a lesson in civic and social duty." The miners were to work during the arbitration period. The breaker whistles blew and the mines reopened on October 23, 1902.

Judge George Gray, who had represented the United States at the Hague Peace Conference, was named Chairman of the commission. The recorder and full member of the commission was Carroll D. Wright, the United States Commissioner of Labor. General John M. Wilson was a member, satisfying the objective that one member be an engineer.

Bishop John L. Spaulding, a member added by Roosevelt, was an outstanding Catholic scholar. Thomas H. Watkins was a former coal operator. Edgar E. Clark, a sociologist, had once been a union official. Edward A. Parker was later to become a publisher of a coal operators' journal. Bishop Spaulding, Clark, and Wright were considered pro-labor. The positions of Chairman Gray and General Wilson were uncertain. Parker and Watkins were considered to be sympathetic to the coal operators.

The commission first heard the case of the miners. The 240 witnesses were brilliantly handled by Attorney Clarence Darrow. Darrow had been hired by Mitchell on the basis of his defense of Eugene Debs and other labor defendants. The witnesses catalogued a series of injustices and hardships that reached the hearts and minds of the world. A typical story related was that of Andrew Chappie, 12 years old, who worked as a breaker boy for forty cents a day. He did not get the money though. It went to pay the debts owed by his father to the coal company, even though Mr. Chappie had been killed in the mines four years earlier. Another was the testimony of Henry Coll, evicted from his home with his 100 year old mother, a sick wife, and a boy adopted when the child's father had been killed in the mines. The family was evicted because Henry Coll had served on a relief committee of striking miners. The night of the eviction, Coll's wife died. The commission hearing the heart-rending testimony pleaded for the end of the horrible narration. From men, women and children, one of whom was just eight years old, the people of the nation and the world got a vivid picture of what it meant to live, work and die in the mining industry.

The important support of the Catholic clergy was obvious to John Mitchell. He knew well the problems that Terence Powderly, a fervent Catholic, had had with clerical misunderstanding and abuse. Mitchell found a real ally in the Reverend John J. Curran of Holy Savior Church in East End, Wilkes-Barre. Curran is credited with advising Mitchell on two major points. Apart from his moral support and lending the strikers the aura of morality, he advised Mitchell against calling out the soft coal miners. Father Curran knew that financial aid was flowing to the anthracite from the soft coal mines, offering some relief to the miners. He felt, too, that a bituminous shutdown would be discouraging rather than encouraging to the anthracite miners.

Father Curran, so effective in molding public opinion, was less successful with the indomitable George Baer. After a conference with the Reading Coal Company magnate, he was compelled to report he found Mr. Baer immovable.

Father Curran also took the stand at the hearings and dispelled the contentions of the operators about miner violence and stressed the eagerness of the miners to return to work. He offered unchallenged testimony that the Wyoming Valley was falsely portrayed to the public.[6]

The coal company spokesmen faced an impossible challenge in formulating their defense against the emotional but concrete testimony prepared by Clarence Darrow for the miners. George Baer, whose arrogant letter had won much public support for the miners, was chief spokesman for the coal operators. Baer did not reply to the testimony of exploitation. Instead, his defense described the law of supply and demand, the rights of management, the dangers to the nation of labor agitation and violence, and the threat of the monopoly of labor in America. At the end of Baer's testimony, he and Mitchell shook hands. This could be viewed as a gesture of fair play, public relations, a Christian's turning the other cheek, or a way of showing even Clarence Darrow that capitalists were human.

Darrow, the thorough lawyer that he was, did not let the testimony of his passionate witnesses stand alone. In an exalted, sublime summation, this nationally known figure,

---

[6] See Chapter VII for additional Curran information.

pouring out the story of the exploitation of the miners, captured the eyes and ears of the nation, saying, in part, "If civilization in this country rests upon the necessity of leaving these starving wages to these miners and laborers . . . to these poor boys who from 12 to 14 are picking their way through the dirt, clouds and dust of the anthracite coal . . . it is time these captains of industry . . . resign their commissions."

The hearing ended and the nation waited for the decision of the committee. Even while they waited, Mitchell was hailed as a hero. When he came to Chicago, 6,000 people met at the Chicago Auditorium to hear him. Also on the platform were 1,100 labor leaders, and as he entered, the band played "Hail the Conquering Hero Comes." The radical left elements were not so enthusiastic. Mitchell was suspect in the eyes of those seeking major changes in the economic system. To them he appeared naive and opportunistic. Even Darrow favored a socialistic economy and John Mitchell had to restrain his lawyer from pleading for such changes.

While a hero among mine workers, Mitchell was attacked by radical reformers and socialists. Mother Jones, the colorful, individualistic figure pleading so often for exploited men, women and children, was especially critical after the strike settlement.

The decision of the arbitration commission came on March 22, 1903. The miners received a ten cent hourly increase in salary, the nine hour day (still not the eight hour day of the bituminous miners) and, most importantly, the creation of a labor-management body for settling disputes. The greatest gain for the coal miners and also for the whole industry was the Anthracite Board of Conciliation made up of six representatives, three from labor, three from mine operators. The Conciliation Board helped keep labor and management at peace over the life of the industry: "The conciliation machinery is the capstone of the government in the industry; it exists . . . affording a just and orderly method for the settlement of disputes, " the arbitration commission emphasized. However it could not prevent all strikes.

The miners did not win a closed shop, but they won partial recognition by the award prohibiting discrimination against union workers. The settlement was a disappointment to many, but not to those most involved. The anthracite miners hailed it as a great victory under a great leader, since they were extremely pleased with the dollar a day increase in pay. Mitchell, while basking in the victory, was aware of the mixed feelings; he noted, "I can never do what people expect of me."

After the 1902 strike ended, newspapers and periodicals designated it as one of the most serious labor conflicts in American history. It had brought President Roosevelt, Clarence Darrow, and a number of well-known political scientists into the anthracite region. Mitchell was then only thirty-three years old. He had raised the dignity, self-esteem, and economic awareness of the mine workers. He had built the United Mine Workers into the single most powerful union in the history of the anthracite area. In doing so, he strengthened the national union in the bituminous regions as well. Ten thousand previously unorganized miners had joined the United Mine Workers, many of whom had been skeptical of the union before Mitchell's success.

In a celebration at the Hotel Hart in Wilkes-Barre on October 26, Mitchell received a citation from Polish, Lithuanian, Ruthenian, and Slavic miners. Its concluding lines were: "Receive, dear leader, a thousand-fold blessing of all the poor, hard-working and struggling people." With the citation came a gold watch and a gold medal similar to the one once given to Lincoln by slaves. The insignia of the United Mine Workers, the pick and shovel crossed above a mine lamp, was engraved in a single mold. John Mitchell's statue on Court House Square in Scranton has a monument as a backdrop. On one side, a quotation from Mitchell is inscribed:

So far as discontent is expressed in constitutional movements for better human betterment, it is health.

On the other side, another quotation reads:

I wish to see the interests and ideals of labor and capital fairly reconciled, not by surrender, but by mutual understanding.

These quotations express Mitchell's belief in reform by constitutional means and his fervent belief that the interests of labor and capital are one. John Mitchell's greatest work was finished by the time he was thirty-three years old.

John Mitchell, hero of the great anthracite strikes of 1900 and 1902, was president of the United Mine Workers from 1898 to 1908.

Date	Day	Name	Occupation	Nationality	Colliery	M./S.	Age	Nature of accident
June	21	Adam Opik	Laborer	Slavonian	Red Ash No. 2	M.	53	Ankle fractured by fall of coal on slope.
	24	Thomas Lally	Engineer	American	Dorrance	M.	50	Legs fractured by being struck by rope on slope.
July	25	Frank Dinlan	Headman	American	Henry	M.	31	Legs fractured by cars on slope.
	1	Joseph Raduts	Laborer	Lithuanian	South Wilkes-Barre No. 5	S.	28	Slightly burned by explosion of gas at face of chamber.
	8	Peter Davitt	Laborer	Polish	South Wilkes-Barre No. 5	M.	47	Toe cut off by piece of failing timber in chamber.
	14	Alexander Munkcul	Miner	Italian	Henry	M.	38	Seriously injured by premature blast at face of chamber.
	25	George Bedwarick	Driver	Polish	Franklin	S.	18	Leg and thigh broken by cars on gangway.
		John Gulunakie	Miner	Polish	Franklin	M.	27	Leg broken by fall of coal at face of chamber.
	29	Mike Hafonto	Loader	Russian	Dorrance	M.	40	Pelvis fractured by cars under breaker. Outside.
Aug.	7	Peter Kochuba	Driver	Polish	Franklin	S.	18	Leg fractured by cars in chamber.
	14	Robert Williams	Miner	Welsh	Hillman Vein	S.	33	Leg fractured by fall of roof at face of chamber.
	22	John Deboah	Miner	Austrian	Hollenback No. 2	S.	27	Slightly burned by explosion of gas at face of chamber.
Sept.	25	Edmund Mullen	Driver	American	Maxwell No. 20	S.	19	Leg fractured by cars at foot of plane.
	29	Edward Smith	Oiler	Irish	Hadleigh	S.	18	Slightly injured by cars on slope.
	15	Joseph Matunic	Bratticeman	Polish	Prospect	S.	32	Slightly burned by explosion of gas in old workings.
		Goulage Hilbire	Assistant foreman	American	Prospect	M.	36	
	25	Peter Nohols	Loader	Russian	Franklin	S.	31	Leg fractured by railroad cars near breaker. Outside.
Oct.	26	Enoch Lavindoakie	Driver	Russian	Prospect	S.	26	Toe crushed by cars at foot of slope.
	2	Vincent Olitski	Footman	Slavonian	Prospect	S.	19	Leg fractured by cars at foot of shaft.
		Mike Switch	Miner	Slavonian	Henry, Luzerne,	M.	26	Arm fractured by explosion of blast at face of chamber.
	13	Hugh Roberts	Miner	Welsh	Maxwell No. 20	M.	40	Leg fractured by explosion of blast at face of chamber.
	27	John Ruddy	Doorboy	American	Prospect	S.	16	Thigh fractured by runaway car on gangway.
		Joseph Zak	Miner	Polish	South Wilkes-Barre No. 5	S.	21	Severely burned by explosion of powder at face of chamber.
Nov.	24	Leo Gorham	Patcher	American	South Wilkes-Barre No. 5	S.	17	Shoulder fractured by cars on gangway.
	25	Adam Studioskie	Laborer	Polish	Henry	S.	52	Leg fractured by cars on gangway.
	27	Nicholas Manaco	Miner	Italian	Franklin	M.	27	Arm fractured by blast at face of chamber.
	3	James Owens	Driver	American	South Wilkes-Barre No. 5	S.	22	Collar bone fractured by cars at foot of shaft.
Dec.	5	J. B. Williams	Engineer	Welsh	South Wilkes-Barre No. 5	M.	36	Hand crushed by cars on gangway.
	10	Stanley Cocheskie	Driver	Polish	Henry	S.	25	Arm fractured by blast at face of chamber.
	19	George Wansack	Driver	Polish	Henry	S.	18	Arm injured by cars on gangway.
	2	Alex Cherbouakia	Miner	Lithuanian	South Wilkes-Barre No. 5	M.	29	Ankle fractured by fall of roof on chamber road.
	10	John C. Thomas	Driver	Welsh	Stanton No. 7	M.	54	Arm fractured by cars at foot of plane.
	16	Charles Waruska	Laborer	Slavonian	Red Ash No. 2	S.	20	Leg fractured by fall of coal on stripping. Outside.
	19	John Haley	Driver	Polish	Miners Mills	S.	23	Seriously injured about body by cars on gangway.

The statistics on mine accidents found in the annual reports of the Pennsylvania Department of Mines included the ethnic origin of the mine workers.

CHAPTER VII

An Irish Priest Befriends Labor

Father John J. Curran

No clerical figure looms larger in anthracite history than Monsignor John J. Curran. In an era when labor was an economic factor equated as property and when equipment and mules were sometimes more valued than immigrant labor, Father Curran gave anthracite miners and their cause a new dignity and status. His crowning achievement was his mediation in the great anthracite coal strike of 1902. His ability to negotiate between such diverse personalities as John Mitchell, George Baer, J. P. Morgan, and President Theodore Roosevelt stamped him as a Christian catalyst.

John Joseph Curran was born in Hawley, Wayne County, Pennsylvania, on June 20, 1859. During his early childhood, his family moved to Avoca in Luzerne County, Pennsylvania. Father Curran's interest in the mines and mining was not merely vicarious. He came from a working-class family, and he himself worked eight years as a breaker boy and as a mule driver. Like hundreds of other youngsters of that era, he became a breaker boy at about eight years of age, was promoted to mule driver, and then left the mines at the age of 16. He became involved in labor history not only as an academic arbitrator, but also as one who had worked in the industry and, as he himself was to attest, as one who had helped to organize a local mining union.

When Curran's family moved to Avoca, he was sixteen years old. At that time, a family decision must have been made that turned him to the priesthood. His education resumed, and John Curran became a student at Wyoming Seminary in Kingston, Pennsylvania. There he earned the equivalent of today's high school education. After graduation, he attended St. Vincent's College at Latrobe, Pennsylvania, and Surpician College of the Grand Seminary in Montreal, Canada. He was ordained at Scranton by Bishiop O'Hara on August 22, 1887, and received his first assignment as an assistant at St. Rose's Church in Carbondale, where he remained eight years.

In 1895, he was assigned to the East End section of Wilkes-Barre. There he organized the Holy Savior Parish, built a church, and remained the spiritual leader of that congregation for twenty-three years. His historical leadership in the anthracite strike of 1902 came while he was pastor of Holy Savior Church.

Father Curran's contribution to the settlement of the 1902 anthracite strike was substantial. He was not merely a token collar-and-gown among warring labor leaders and mine operators. He was a day-by-day, month-by-month worker, carrying out a strenuous campaign of leg work, letter writing, and conferences. The Reverend John P. Gallagher wrote in his history of the Scranton Diocese, that the greatest contribution of Father Curran was giving respectability to the cause of the strikers and in creating for them a positive public image. That achievement was possible only because Father Curran knew the economic needs of the miners, the objectives of the mine operators, and the dependence of the consumers. Above all, he was willing and able to lend weeks of arduous effort to pleading, conciliating, and interpreting the mission of John Mitchell and the mine workers.

Typical of Father Curran's indefatigable work was his personal mission to the mine operators. When John Mitchell set up his headquarters at the Hotel Hart on East Market Street in Wilkes-Barre, the place where the Federal Building now stands, Father Curran was in constant communication with him. These meetings led Father Curran on a campaign

98

to convince capital to negotiate a settlement of the impasse. Sister Mary Annunciata Merrick, R.S.M., a niece of Father Curran, in her doctoral dissertation on the strike of 1902, enumerates these efforts: Father Curran spent two hours trying to convince the recalcitrant George Baer, spokesman for the coal operators, and author of the famous "divine-right letter," to meet with John Mitchell. Unsuccessful with Mr. Baer, he pressed on to President Olyphant of the Delaware, Lackawanna and Western Railroad. Again unsuccessful, he went on to meet with the captain of industry himself, Mr. John Pierpont Morgan. Curran found that although Morgan favored meeting Mitchell, he deferred to Baer. When these conciliatory trips failed, and with the nation suffering deprivation and cold from the fuel shortage, Father Curran called at the White House and, in pleading the cause of the anthracite miners, met President Theodore Roosevelt. Immediately, a bond was established between them, a bond which lasted their lifetimes. Of their friendships, Teddy Roosevelt wrote in his autobiography: "The man in Wilkes-Barre who helped me the most was Father Curran. I grew to know and trust and believe in him, and throughout my term in office and afterward, he was not only my staunch friend, but one of the men by whose advice and counsel I profited most in matters affecting the welfare of miners and their families." Lest this be interpreted as perfunctory thanks, the content of a number of letters between the President and the priest reveal Roosevelt's warm feelings. Roosevelt wrote: "No man has ever had a stauncher friend than you have been to me. You have supported me in every way . . . There is no friend . . . in whose friendship I take greater pride than yours."

The bond of friendship was cemented by Father Curran's expert testimony before the Roosevelt Anthracite Committee. Roosevelt, after applying persistent pressure on mine owners and miners, was able to convince the coal operators to agree to arbitrate the issues at stake in the strike. The miners went back to work and the Committee opened hearings in Washington, Scranton, and Wilkes-Barre.

The Committee produced 10,047 legal pages. Five hundred and fifty witnesses were heard, and the hearings were prime national news for weeks. Father Curran was undoubtedly one of the most effective in presenting the causes of the miners. Prodded by Clarence Darrow, the brilliant socially-conscious attorney chosen to present the case of the workers, Father Curran helped to dispel the notion that some of the miners were anti-Mitchell for not really representing the rank and file worker. An article in Collier's Magazine had claimed that the coal magnates were insisting that Mitchell was an agitator without support of the majority of the miners. An exchange in the witness stand produced the following: Clarence Darrow, pointing to the picture of alleged anti-Mitchell workers, asked Curran, "Do you know who got these people to pose?"

"Collier's Magazine," Father Curran replied.

"Who is the man at the head of the picture? Do you know him?" asked Darrow.

Father Curran: "Yes, sir. His name is Will McGroarty and he is the biggest striker we have. He posed as a scab."

The courtroom rang with laughter.

Apart from his yeoman work as conciliator, negotiator, and witness for the miners, Father Curran provided additional service with his personal economic and psychological advice to John Mitchell. Curran was one who is credited with advising Mitchell not to call out the bituminous coal workers. He knew that a bituminous coal strike would discourage the miners of western Pennsylvania, Kentucky and West Virginia and, even more importantly, it would cut off financial aid from the soft coal fields. There is little doubt that the charismatic priest was responsible, in large part, for the favorable and historic decision of the Roosevelt arbitration commission.

100

The association of Father Curran and President Theodore Roosevelt begun during the Anthracite Strike of 1902, warmed over the years. The climax of their friendship occurred on August 21, 1912, the day when Roosevelt opened his presidential campaign as the Bull Moose Party candidate against President Taft and Woodrow Wilson. The campaign started with a mass rally at Holy Savior Church in East End. There Bishop Michael J. Hoban and seventy priests of the Scranton diocese along with a crowd of 10,000 welcomed the jubilant Roosevelt. A mass and an evening dinner at Harvey's Lake capped a day often overlooked in Wyoming Valley history.

Father Curran, known primarily as a social activist, was also a tireless, efficient administrator. After his appointment by Bishop Hoban as irremovable pastor of St. Mary's Church, he presided over a congregation which frequently served ten thousand worshipers on Sundays. He was responsible for the administrative changes leading to the establishment of St. Patrick's Church in the Rolling Mill Hill section of Wilkes-Barre, of St. Therese's in South Wilkes-Barre and St. John's in North Wilkes-Barre. He was also a prime mover in the creation of College Misericordia.

In 1930, he was invested as Monsignor Curran. As his career progressed, his activities increased. He promoted playgrounds, aid to the blind, and was an inveterate letter writer to presidents, popes, and government officials of every rank. He was appointed by Governor Fisher to represent Pennsylvania at the World Congress Against Alcoholism.

Monsignor Curran, brought into the limelight by his support of the anthracite miners in 1902, ended his career in much the same way. In 1934, a new union, the United Anthracite Miners of Pennsylvania sprouted in Wyoming Valley. Rebelling against the bureaucracy of the national United Mine Workers and its preoccupation with the bituminous coal fields, the new union hoped to succeed through New Deal legislation.

The new union triggered a period of violent rivalry between its factions and members of the United Mine Workers. Monsignor Curran's role was one of peacemaker in the quarrel. Undoubtedly the new union would have been crushed as a dissident upstart had not Monsignor Curran made numerous trips to Washington on its behalf. These trips tired him, but he was adamant in his desire to solve the grievances of all anthracite miners. As the National Labor Relations Board was ready to terminate the strike in favor of the powerful United Mine Workers, Monsignor Curran produced 100,000 signatures petitioning for an equitable solution. Reminiscent of 1902, thirty-two years earlier, twelve hundred United Anthracite Miners honored Monsignor Curran for his efforts at a rally in the South Main Street Armory. The United Anthracite Workers were elated, believing Monsignor Curran had won their cause.

An agreement was made between the quarreling unions to have James A. Gorman of Hazleton, a member of the Anthracite Conciliation Board, appointed as the sole arbitrator of grievances. The United Anthracite Miners rallied in a full-force demonstration, 25,000 strong at Kirby Park, Wilkes-Barre, on Labor Day 1934, confident of victory. But after forty-five days of hearings in Scranton, Gorman, assisted by Dr. Thomas Larkin and Dr. Charles P. Neill, produced several decisions against the United Anthracite Workers of Pennyslvania.

The decisions of Umpire Gorman were crushing blows to the new anthracite union, and the members were reluctant to accept the decisions. Men refused to work. The Gorman decisions ended their confidence. Violence continued during the early winter. In February 1935, Judge Valentine issued an injunction against the new union to desist from violence and to stop interfering with other working men who were loyal to the United Mine Workers. In spite of the court order, violence continued. The Delaware, Lackawanna and Western Railroad bridge was dynamited.

The Glen Alden Coal Company, whose production suffered from the conflict between the old and new unions, instituted court action against Thomas Maloney, president of the new union, and forty-nine others. At the court hearing on March 14, 1935, the supporters of the new union nearly stampeded the court room. When Maloney and twenty-eight others said they would refuse to recognize a court order even if it were issued by the Supreme Court of Pennsylvania, they were put in prison. They remained there for one month and were released on April 18, when the new union's officers agreed to abide by court decisions.

The United Anthracite Miners of Pennsylvania was in its last days. The strength of the United Mine Workers, the opposition of the major coal companies, and the adverse decisions of Judge James A. Gorman, the arbitrator, were too much. Even the intercession of Monsignor Curran was to no avail. The great labor priest was able to get the new union a hearing, but the forces of power and decision were elsewhere. Facing defeat, Thomas Maloney tried a peace proposal. Instead of peace, a new wave of violence erupted at many collieries as members of the rival factions, ignoring the decisions, opposed each other with physical violence and dynamite bombings. Even after the legal disbanding of the new union in October 1935, violence still continued.

But the violence of the strike paled in comparison to the shock-wave that went through Wyoming Valley on Good Friday, April 10, 1936. On that day, six well-wrapped cigar boxes filled with dynamite were mailed indiscriminately to homes of public figures. Efforts to link the bombings to the union warfare were not successful as some of the victims favored the new union, others opposed it, and some had no apparent connection to the chaotic violence. Thomas Maloney and a four year old son were killed. Another Maloney child, sixteen year old Margaret, was badly injured and hospitalized for several months. The boxes sent to Gorman and several others were intercepted, and those lives spared. Also killed was Michael Gallagher, the sexton of St. Mary's Cemetery. His son-in-law, Clinton Lehman, a school teacher, was badly injured. Others intended but spared were Judge Benjamin R. Jones, Luzerne County Sheriff Luther Kniffen, and Henry Goulstone, superintendent of the Buttonwood Colliery of the Glen Alden Coal Company. One Michael Fugman, a former sergeant in the German Imperial Artillery, was arrested for the crimes, tried, convicted, and put to death in the electric chair. His motivation for the crime was never established as his victims and intended victims were a diverse group.

The violence of the strike itself, and the horror of the Easter bombings shocked Monsignor Curran, the prelate of forty-nine years' service. The afternoon of the bombings, a fire broke out in St. Mary's rectory destroying his prized historical possessions. On Easter Monday, he suffered a heart attack and remained in critical condition for months. On November 8, 1936, Monsignor Curran died; he was buried on Armistice Day, with thousands attending his funeral. The venerable prelate was eulogized as "a friend of Presidents, advisor of labor, confidante of authorities and benefactor of humanity."

The life and career of Monsignor John J. Curran, like that of the great ecumenist Pope John XXIII of the twentieth century, reflected the empathy of one born in a humble working-class family. Following the injunction of Christ to heal, to preach, to teach, Monsignor Curran moved among his people interpreting love in service and action. Just as Reinhold Niebuhr was later to work among auto workers in Detroit, the former breaker boy devoted his life to the amelioration of pain among people struggling with problems of a new economic period. He brought dignity and respect to the workers in the coal-mining industry. Through him, the immigrant miners saw the real promises of America.

On August 21, 1912, President Theodore Roosevelt opened his Bull Moose campaign with Bishop Hoban, Father Curran, and a crowd of 10,000 at Holy Savior Roman Catholic Church in East End, Wilkes-Barre. Roosevelt said of Father Curran: "My staunch friend . . . one by whose counsel I profited most in matters affecting miners and their families."

CHAPTER VIII

A Slavic Inferno

Baltimore Tunnel Explosion, 1919

Young Jim Gillespie, in East End, Wilkes-Barre, heard his father downstairs preparing to go to work at the Baltimore Colliery. Although it was early morning, the sun was streaming in Jim's bedroom. The school year was coming to an end, but on this June 5th summer morning, Jim remembered he had not been in school the previous day and needed a written excuse from home about that absence. He jumped out of bed, but his father had already gone out the kitchen door. Undaunted, he ran down to the kitchen in a moment and opened the kitchen door, yelling, "Dad, Dad, I need an excuse." Jim's dad returned patiently, complied with his son's need and started once more for work.

As he hurried to the mine, he was aware that the delay in writing the excuse might have caused him to miss his ride into the mine. For the working miner, there are two ways to enter a mine. The first is by cage, or crude elevator, that plummets hundreds of feet in seconds. The second is by way of a slope. Men sometimes walk down the slopes, but usually, especially in a deep mine where the slope was long and distant, they would pile into empty cars being hauled into the mine at the beginning of the work day. Frequently, the day's supplies, including blasting powder, were loaded on the cars with the men.

When Mr. Gillespie got to the mine, a trip loaded with men and powder was disappearing into the earth. He had missed his ride into the mine. He was very upset. He would have to wait for the next trip. Within moments, an explosive blast shook the mine and the whole East End of Wilkes-Barre trembled. The trip of coal cars that Jim's father had missed was loaded with men; several of the cars were loaded with boxes of powder for the day's mining. Inexplicably, the powder had ignited, setting off an explosion that killed 92 men. This disaster, fifty years after the one at Avondale, and twenty-five years after the Irish tragedy at Pittston's Twin Shaft, showed again that despite progress and improvement of safety regulations, mining remained a dangerous, deadly industry.

The horror of the explosion and fire was vividly described by three survivors. One was Jacob Milz, an elderly tracklayer employed for over 40 years in or around the mines. On the morning of the disaster, he rode into the mine on the first car behind the motor (engine) pulling fourteen coal cars carrying 150 men. After the explosion, Milz escaped injury by jumping from the first car and crawling on his knees 200 feet into the mine, into an area known as the G vein, a clear section with good circulating air. As he described his experience, his underplayed heroism became apparent:

"I really don't know what happened until the trip came to a stop. . . . I had about three miles to go when the trip stopped. All the working men (in the cars) were in good spirits and they talked, laughed and joked with each other. Presently the trip stopped and everything seemed to be enveloped in a smoky haze. In the rear, I heard men coughing, then suddenly shrieking and groaning. Every second the smoke became more dense. Agonizing shrieks were heard on all sides and the men in the car with me started to climb out. My throat was parched. I coughed and sputtered and clambered over the cars. In my anxiety, for everybody was scrambling to get out first, I fell, but I quickly regained my feet and started through the tunnel. The tunnel was full of smoke. I couldn't see and I dropped to my hands and knees. I really can't say now how I managed to escape all that. All I remember is that I kept crawling for the longest time till I

107

reached the G vein. It seemed to me like years, and from every part came loud shrieks of agony and pain. When I reached G vein several had gotten there before me. My throat and lungs cleared and no one spoke. Solemn silence reigned for a few minutes when I jumped up and said, 'Come on boys, we boys have work to do.' I don't know how many were there but there wasn't one slacker in the crowd. All of them jumped to their feet, discarded coats and hats, tied handkerchiefs around faces and nostrils and we started the work of rescue. I don't want any credit for my part. I thank God that I am safe and my heart goes out to the unfortunate comrades of mine that lost their lives. If I have saved a single life, I feel repaid a thousand times because God in all his infinite mercy saved mine. I don't know how many men I helped carry out but I worked hard for the longest time and then I weakened. I am not a young man any more and the bodies of the men were heavy."

While the interview with Mr. Jacob Milz described some of the terror, it remained for Mr. John McGroarty to provide more details of the Baltimore Tunnel tragedy. He was the motorman driving the engine into the mine of the Baltimore Tunnel. He testified before the Chief of the Pennsylvania Bureau of Mines, Steward Button, and several inspectors of the department and officials of the Delaware and Hudson Coal Company. McGroarty stated that he had taken the fourteen car trip loaded with 150 miners only a short distance into the mine, the last car being only about 175 feet from the entry, when he was stopped by four men exiting. The four men said the trolley, conductor of electricity for the engine, had fallen from its bracket and should be repaired. McGroarty and his brakeman, James Kehoe, uncoupled the engine from the fourteen cars and informed the men they would have to walk in. McGroarty and Kehoe then drove the engine alone about 50 feet and found the fallen bracket. They were just about to inform the switchman to turn off the electricity so they could repair the bracket when they saw a sheet of flame and a cloud of smoke behind them. About two minutes had elapsed between their uncoupling of the motor and their observation of flame and smoke.

Obviously from the recollection of Jacob Milz some of the men had not yet left the cars. As reported, Jacob Milz in one of the front cars crawled to G vein. McGroarty, Kehoe, and the four exiting men immediately ran back to help those seared by the flames or choked by the black smoke. The rescuers carried man after man back to G vein. All worked feverishly with handkerchiefs over their mouths and nostrils. Once, almost overcome, McGroarty dipped his face in the small stream running along the tracks. Later he collapsed completely and did not recover until he awoke in a hospital bed.

Jim Kehoe, the brakeman, related the most horrible story. He told of fighting the choking smoke and instead of dragging men toward G vein, worked toward the entrance. He came upon the area of the mine cars closest to the dynamite car and found men "being roasted alive." He tried to pull one out and skin and clothes together pulled away from the body. He continued toward the entry, fell over the body, yet alive, of a well-known amateur baseball player, Jim McCloskey, who was frightfully burned, with his tongue so swollen that he could not talk, although he made an effort to do so. He said he took hold of him and attempted to carry him out but he was unable to proceed with him. He said the man was near death but had enough strength to give him his brotherhood book and papers in it. At this point McCloskey became delirious and grabbed Kehoe by the throat and it was with considerable effort that he was able to pry the man's fingers loose. After freeing himself he again made an effort to get out of the place, when he came to a heap of dead and dying men, piled four feet high, many of them with their clothes on fire. He crawled around them and in doing so his shirt caught fire. This he jerked from his body, and soon began to inhale fresh air, and yelled to those ahead of him

109

asking how far he was from the mouth of the tunnel. A voice answered, 'not far' and with a superhuman effort he reached fresh air and safety."

The same reporter described Kehoe's exit as seen by those outside: "Kehoe came reeling out of the tunnel naked to the waist while startled men stood looking at him in fear. He screamed to them to go inside and help with the work of rescue and when he rushed back in they followed him and the work of bringing out the dead and dying started in earnest, and it was not long before all were removed."

Late in the evening of June 5, 1919, additional facts emerged surrounding the disastrous trip which had started into the mine early that morning at 6:50 a.m. The creek running along the track was deemed to be two feet deep. Many of the victims, either seeking refuge from burns, or perhaps blown into it, had drowned. Bodies were piled high in the water.

Two days after the tragic disaster, Saturday, June 7, Steward Button, Chief of the Pennsylvania Department of Mines, called a conference at the colliery. Button announced an investigation by national mine experts plus a special committee of local mine inspectors, chaired by Joseph J. Walsh. After the conference, Button released his findings and a list of possible causes of the explosion. The exact cause of the explosion was never determined. Speculation pointed to the ignition of the powder by a short-circuited wire, a miner's crow-bar touching an overhead wire, or a spark from one of the open-flame lamps still being used. The latter was discounted by the investigators. A number of defective cans of powder were found in the colliery storage houses. Seven cans of unexploded powder were inexplicably in the front cars of the trip. The conclusion was that the cans which had exploded also were defective. The public was appalled and shocked by the accident, especially by the transportation of men and explosives together.

In reviewing the possible causes of the accident, testimony revealed that in August 1918, the union had won the right

110

for miners to be transported into the mines. The miners seeking this transportation were pursuing a grievance which had plagued mine workers for generations. They often had to walk treacherous miles underground before arriving at their place of work. The company responded by agreeing to provide one trip of cars for the men each morning. However, it was stipulated that powder was to be transported only in the last car with the car directly in front of the last to be unoccupied.

The devastating explosion of the Baltimore Tunnel of the No. 5 Colliery of the Delaware and Hudson Coal Company came during the peak year of anthracite production. The 92 men killed were among 556 other men killed that year when nearly 100 million tons of anthracite were mined. The 92 men killed were predominantly Polish, Lithuanian, Slovak, and Russian, with a smaller number of Irish, Welsh, Scotch and English, a direct reflection of the ethnic changes which had occurred over the years in the anthracite region.

Words and picture stories of 1919 portrayed the poignant sorrow and cruel ravages of the calamity. Especially vivid was the picture of a common funeral Mass at St. Mary's Polish Catholic Church on Park Avenue, Wilkes-Barre, with rows of caskets in the aisles. Many of the victims were buried in a common grave in the parish cemetery in the Georgetown section of Wilkes-Barre Township. The widows, children, sweethearts, neighbors, and friends of these victims suffered no less than survivors of other disasters; however, the financial suffering was mitigated by payments in the form of workmen's compensation. The work of John Siney, Terence Powderly, John Mitchell and many other men of social-consciousness had established a workmen's compensation fund, as well as greater justice in pay and working hours. Too, on the scene, the Salvation Army and Red Cross were visible, offering some measures of relief. In addition, the investigation following the disaster was evidence of a more civilized concern. In fact, accounts of the investigations of

111

A funeral Mass for many of the victims of the Baltimore Tunnel Explosion was held at St. Mary's Polish Catholic Church, Park Avenue, Wilkes-Barre. Most of the victims were immigrants from Eastern European nations.

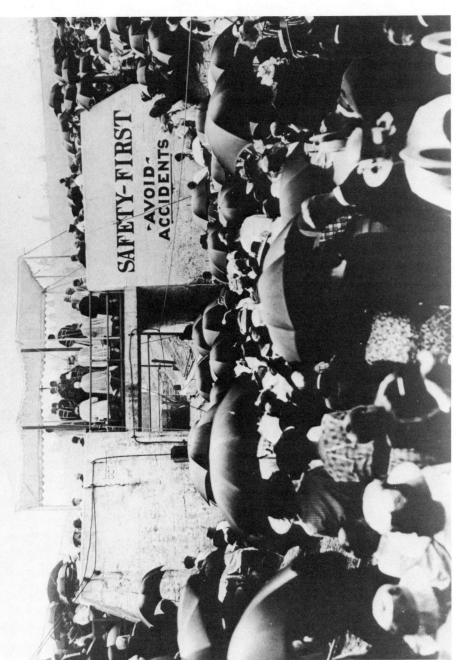

A special Mass was offered at the head of Baltimore Tunnel in East End, Wilkes-Barre, for the 92 workers killed the morning of June 5, 1919.

the mining disaster reveal that by 1919, the unions as well as the state tried to supplement workers' compensation with additional relief.

Nevertheless, despite the industrial growth of the nation between the post-Civil War era and the post-World War I era, and despite a more sensitive and responsible society, the miner was still at the mercy of explosions, falling roofs, methane gas poisoning, and other lethal threats. If a miner managed to survive these threats and hazards, he still lived with lungs so filled with silica that there was no easing of his long last mile. Death at an early age came from anthra-silicosis, called black lung by most miners.

The Avondale Disaster in 1869, had inspired Terence Powderly to become the national leader of the Knights of Labor. The Twin Shaft disaster of 1896, helped to set the stage for the emergence of a new force on the labor front, the force embodied in John Mitchell and his work in the United Mine Workers Union. After the Baltimore Tunnel Explosion of 1919, a new figure appeared on the labor scene. His face was to appear over and over in newspapers and magazines and newsreels for the next thirty years; the face was that of John Llewellyn Lewis.

CHAPTER IX

The Welsh Contradiction

John L. Lewis, a Republican Labor Giant

From the time of the great anthracite strike of 1902 until the year 1913, there was little progress made in improving safety measures or working conditions in the mines, and wages rose little. In 1906, miners earned about $785 a year. During the period from 1902 to 1922, the basic wage increases came as a result of the awards of the Anthracite Commission set up after the great 1902 strike. It was not until 1922 that the anthracite miners launched another campaign to improve their conditions, this time under their new leader.

In 1922, the new leader was a hulking Welshman, John L. Lewis, a leader with whom the miners of the anthracite region were to have a love–hate relationship for over forty years. Until 1936, when the Congress of Industrial Organization was created, miners regarded Lewis as the typical arrogant bureaucrat. Even in 1936, when he was praised by Heywood Hale Broun, Marquis Childs, and other liberal writers, the anthracite miners were skeptical. Lewis came out of Southern Iowa, not the beautiful flat farm lands, but an area more like neighboring Missouri, with numerous coal camp towns. His parents had migrated from the coal-mining area of South Wales and more than likely spoke Welsh in the family circle. Married in Lucas, Iowa in 1878, soon after their migration, the Lewises first child, John Llewellyn Lewis was born on February 12, 1880, the birthday anniversary of Abraham Lincoln.

Lewis' uncertain popularity in the anthracite region was due in no small measure to his geographical alienation. He was always a soft-coal man. His years of organizing with the United Mine Workers had covered the western and central states and Appalachia. Lewis was a scowling, intense, formidable man and, accordingly, "the most visible sight in the nation's capital, next to the Washington Monument." One could have added, "and just as cold." Miners thought of him as something of a character. If he got what they wanted, they gave him his due, but barely. Lewis and his bureaucratic organization engendered much of this alienation and uncertainty. He ruled with an iron hand and the district chairmen imitated him. The typical local union in the anthracite area was dominated by an oligarchy. Very little democracy existed anywhere in the anthracite districts of the U.M.W. under John L. Lewis.

Lewis, in his later attitudes and ambitions, was light-years away from the anthracite miners. If the accounts of his private life are accurate, his interest in banking, his propensity to socialize only with prestigious people in Washington, his interest in acquiring wealth and living in the style of the Alexandria set, then he certainly did not live on common ground with coal miners. This arrogant, soft-coal man stepped into the anthracite picture in 1922. The anthracite workers wanted to eliminate the wage differentials between the hard and soft-coal miners, and especially between day-laborers. Laborers in the anthracite mines received from two to three dollars a day less than the soft-coal laborers. Lewis wanted a check-off, a company collection of union dues, and the closed shop. The closed shop barred mine employment to non-union members. The mine operators postponed negotiations as long as possible. Lewis, at the expiration of the old contract, called a strike. The strike lasted only six days. The settlement came out of a meeting between the union and operators in Harrisburg. The meeting was urged and supported by Governor Pinchot and President Coolidge. Lewis did not attend the negotiations. Absent because of illness, he sent Phil Murray to represent him. After a short, six day strike, an agreement was signed giving all mine workers a 10 per cent increase in wages. The much sought after check-off system was unrealized; dues still were to be collected by the union. In turn, the operators, fearing oil and gas competition, agreed to only small increases in coal prices.

Three years later, in 1925, Lewis again approached the operators with some proposals. He did not want a strike, but he was still adamant about a check-off system which would use the company to collect union dues.He also hoped to get a long-term contract. He met with the operators in Atlantic City while his family enjoyed the summer vacation. The miners in the Valley watched and listened, but continued to work during the summer while enjoying their summer daylight evening hours gardening, fishing, doing home repairs, and getting caught up with other work. Lewis could not believe it when in July, the operators refused his proposals. He refused arbitration, saying what capital and labor understood only too well: ask for arbitration when you're weak, refuse it when you're strong. He waited for government pressure on the operators.

When it did not come, he called the miners out on September 1. More than 150,000 miners struck in what became the longest strike in anthracite history, even exceeding the 1902 stoppage. The strike marked the beginning of the depression for the anthracite area. While the nation enjoyed the prosperity of the late twenties, the anthracite regions, in the winter of 1925–1926, had a taste of what they and the rest of the nation would experience in the 1930's.

In the midst of the strike, Lewis went back to his main concern, the soft-coal region. As he worked to consolidate and organize, he was hit with an avalanche of court injunctions. One of them attacked the miners, accusing them of threatening men who wanted to work by demeaning them as scabs. Worse, the miners were accused of intimating murder when they sang, "shoot them in the head, shoot them in the feet, shoot them in the dinner bucket, how are they

117

going to eat?" Lewis also was served with several injunctions which he treated, as one of his aides put it, like "leaves of grass."

In the midst of frustration and quarrels with Coolidge and Hoover over the Federal obligation in the dispute, Lewis turned back to the union security stronghold, the anthracite areas. There he found the operators and miners exhausted and ready for peace. The settlement was not a great victory, pointing to yet another source of the anthracite miners' indifference to Lewis, indifference particularly strong among the rank and file. Lewis never seemed to produce a real victory for hard-coal miners. The settlement gave the miners a five-year contract. Most of the celebrating was at the signing of the agreement at the Bellevue-Stratford in Philadelphia on February 12, Lincoln's birthday anniversary and Lewis' 46th birthday. W. W. Ingliss, a coal operator, gave Lewis a basket of roses. Miners would have preferred a better contract. Lewis had even failed to get his check-off. The check-off, company collection of union dues, was not won until 1941.

Although wages were set, there was very little else about which to cheer. There was no doubt that gas and oil were supplanting hard coal as a source of fuel. During the strike, many home-owners and industries were caught in a bind and converted to the newer fuels. The anthracite strike of 1925 was blamed in part for the loss of many of the last markets for anthracite. Coal operators found it difficult to compete against gas and oil in an open market. In addition, coal was suspect because of the industry's volatile labor-management relationship. Added to the instability were outdated and unimaginative sales methods and the absence of research. As a result of oil and gas competition, coal production fell from a peak of 99 million tons in 1917 to an annual production of 68 million tons between 1926 and 1930. *The Nation* reported, ". . . anthracite is a . . . sick industry."

During the years from 1925 to 1929, while the nation was occupied with flappers, bathtub-gin, the Charleston, Black Bottom, and Varsity Drag, thousands of anthracite coal miners lived through a hectic economic period. In Wyoming Valley, the heart of the anthracite region, a great exodus began—to Ohio, Michigan, Connecticut and New Jersey. This exodus slackened somewhat in the pre-World War II days and then exploded again in the 1940's and 1950's as unemployment again spread in the anthracite region. But before the post World War II exodus, the nation was to see and hear much more of John L. Lewis, the tough, flamboyant Welsh egotist who, when talking to cynical Washington newsmen, could begin a statement with, "methinks . . ." and get way with it. Regardless of his language, he was always good copy.

Better days were to come in the anthracite area. Hoover was succeeded by Franklin Delano Roosevelt. Lewis and other labor leaders took heart when Roosevelt's New Deal included the National Labor Relations Act. The New Deal was started in 1933 and by 1934 had developed programs spearheading recovery. Among those programs was a labor Magna Carta opening new doors for collective bargaining. For Lewis, it was an unprecedented opportunity for organizing miners. The years between 1932 and 1940 marked the height of his popularity.[1] And at no time and nowhere was this more apparent than on October 29, 1936, in Wilkes-Barre, Pennsylvania, when Lewis rode into town in style with Roosevelt to celebrate the anniversary of the ending of the 1900 strike, not the 1902 strike as many believe. It was Johnny Mitchell Day.

The Pennsylvania Railroad's special train carried Roosevelt and Lewis on a spur line into Miner Park, in the southern

---

[1] The year 1934 also marked the low point of Lewis' popularity in the anthracite region. See Chapter VII for an account of the revolt of anthracite mine workers through the United Anthracite Workers of Pennsylvania.

119

end of the city, where the anticipated crowd could be massed in an open area. The train had come through Mauch Chunk, to Wilkes-Barre, to the Buttonwood section of Hanover Township, and then on the spur into Miner Park. As it passed through Hanover Township, in the early morning, thousands lined the tracks to cheer. By 9 a.m., the train was stopped at Miner Park where a crowd, variously estimated from 35,000 to 75,000 people, jammed the field. A cheer went up when a floral piece, a miner's mule made from 4,000 red and white carnations, was sighted on the speaker's platform. John L. Lewis had the honor of introducing the President. Lewis, rarely seen in the anthracite area, seemed content to bask in the Mitchell heritage and the Roosevelt charisma. He introduced Roosevelt with a few succinct paragraphs. The President in turn began his remarks by saying, ". . . I realized it was John Mitchell Day. I was determined to come to Wilkes-Barre. I want to pay tribute to one I was happy to call a friend." He went on to recount how John Mitchell had saved the country thousands of dollars during World War I in the purchase of coal, how he, Roosevelt, as assistant secretary of the navy, had used the advice of John Mitchell. After lauding Mitchell, he gave a ringing political address, flaying employers for their opposition to the great new legislation of his New Deal, the Social Security Act.

John L. Lewis, at the height of his popularity, with the charismatic Roosevelt at his side, all under the cloak and mantle of the revered John Mitchell, still seemed to be uncertain of and lacking confidence in Wyoming Valley. Nevertheless, Lewis "politicked" in Wilkes-Barre for Roosevelt, and did so unreservedly throughout the country. More importantly, he donated and loaned the Democratic Party almost a half-million dollars of union funds, equal to several million in today's economy. The money supported the party which was responsible for opening the doors of union organization. The Democratic Party was paving the way for a new type of labor industrial organization and structure.

In 1936, John L. Lewis seemed to emerge as a new progressive labor leader. He saw changing needs in the field of labor and began the tremendous organization of workers into industrial unions. He saw the end of the typical craft unions unable to cope with or combat the trusts and corporations of an industrial America. His vision was a Congress of Industrial Organization to pull steel workers, auto workers, coal miners, and a host of other organized groups under one unified banner. His clarion call to workers everywhere was: "The labor movement is organized upon a principle that the strong shall help the weak. To increase union membership, organizers exploited the President's sympathies, saying, "The President wants you to join the union." As expected, new memberships exploded into thousands.

The real test which Lewis faced on the road to converting his vision into reality came at the American Federation of Labor convention in Atlantic City in 1936. The A. F. of L. was packed with pro-craft union labor bureaucrats. Lewis still hoped to build an industrial organization with the A. F. of L. In language typical of Lewis, he argued: ". . . the craft union . . . may stand like mighty oaks before the gale, defy the lightning . . . yet the day may come . . . when they may not. Now prepare . . . heed this cry from Macedonia." Despite his flowery plea, Lewis lost the first vote, 18,024 to 10,993.

Undaunted, three days later he electrified the nation with the battle of Atlantic City. The convention was still in session when Big Bill Hutchinson, a leader of the carpenters, a craft union, became annoyed by an industrial union speaker and called for a point of order. Lewis jumped up defending the speaker, saying the point of order was small potatoes. Hutchinson weighed 300 pounds, a giant of a man like Lewis himself, said loudly, "I was raised on small potatoes; that's why I'm so small." In a moment, the two men were heatedly arguing as they had a hundred times in the past. These two behemoths were former poker-playing cronies, leaders in

A. F. of L. strategy, but at that moment, Hutchinson and Lewis were opponents. Hutchinson stood for craft unions characterized by the business-agent approach to organization. Suddenly, the argument between the two men exploded, and the word "bastard" was heard. Lewis threw a punch which caught Hutchinson on the face. Blows were exchanged and the two giants tumbled over the platform chairs. According to Lewis, the fight was pre-ordained.

Before the convention was ended, Lewis called supportive union leaders to a breakfast. There they formed a Committee for Industrial Organization as part of the A. F. of L. and appointed Lewis as the committee's president. The battle of Atlantic City was over. It was hailed by liberals as a victory and a new day for effective democratic unionization. Heywood Broun wrote a column in the *New Republic* in which he noted that when John Lewis knocked down Big Bill Hutchinson, he struck a blow long to be remembered in American Labor history. Broun called Lewis "the greatest heavyweight of our time," comparing him with fighter Joe Louis for his great strength among the workers.

The battle might have been over, but there was still no peace in sight. The C.I.O. was still part of the A. F. of L. While Lewis did not have the votes at the A. F. of L. convention to make it an industrial rather than a craft union, there was no denying that his control of the United Mine Workers was intact. There also was no denying the U.M.W. support of industrial unionization. Nowhere was this more apparent than at the next convention of the United Mine Workers, when John Lewis challenged William Green, the president of the A. F. of L. Green was the A. F. of L. president, but held this position because he was an officer of the United Mine Workers. He appeared before the miners' convention pleading to the workers to forget the insanity of industrial organization. The man to whom Lewis had poured out his vision a year earlier, who then might have said "take it easy," was now in full opposition to the C.I.O. When he had finished, Lewis called for a standing vote of Green's supporters. Allegedly, only one of the 2,000 delegates rose. Immediately, Green was suspended. He was without portfolio in the A. F. of L., even though he was president. That situation was corrected when James Caesar Petrillo gave Green a card in the musician's union.

Following this action, the C.I.O. withdrew as a committee within the A. F. of L. and became an independent structure. The split occurred officially on August 4, 1936. The United States had two major competing labor forces, the C.I.O., Congress of Industrial Organization, and the A. F. of L., the American Federation of Labor.

For eight years, from 1932 to 1940, Lewis was loyal to Roosevelt and the Democratic Party. Lewis supported both with huge sums of money. But, by 1940, Lewis had become disillusioned. The reasons were manifold. In short, the temperament, egos, and power rivalries of both men made the alliance untenable. As the election of 1940 approached, Lewis made an historical pronouncement, the ringing pronouncement that if Roosevelt won, he, Lewis, would resign his C.I.O. office. Roosevelt did win the election and Lewis lived up to his promise. To the amazement of the public, he severed his ties with the C.I.O.

At the convention in Atlantic City just weeks after Roosevelt's victory, Lewis stood before the C.I.O. delegates and fulfilled his pledge, dramatically using prose, poetry, and platitudes, sprinkled sometimes with brilliant allusions and sometimes with vague references, but at all times in commanding splendor. His speech ended with real tears. "I won't be with you long . . . Do not trouble yourselves. That is the way of life . . . the heights are cold." And then, directly quoting, "Who ascends the mountain top finds the loftiest peaks encased in . . . mist and snow. . . . He shortly turns from the well who drinks his fill and the squeezed orange falls from the golden salver to the dung." The Lewis rhetoric was in full swing. Ironically, the left-wing, Communist-dom-

123

inated unions, along with loyalists, pleaded with him to stay. The Hitler-Stalin pact was in force and the Communists were strongly anti-war and anti-Roosevelt. However, the host of liberals who supported Roosevelt did not object to the resignation. With his friend Phil Murray succeeding him, Lewis returned to the secure throne of the United Mine Workers and the imperial presidency of "his own" union in sumptuous new headquarters, not in sooty Indianapolis, but in the nation's capital, Washington, D.C.

The stage was set for the World War II Roosevelt-Lewis confrontation. Although Lewis had elaborate new offices, he lacked the support of former union allies and liberal friends. Nevertheless, as president of the U.M.W., he held a most powerful position in a nation facing a prolonged war. Coal was a crucial commodity to a wartime economy.

By 1940, the coal miners of America, and the anthracite miners in particular, were once again enjoying a full workweek. The depression was over. "Bundles for Britain" included anthracite coal for the Allies. In 1941 Lewis finally won the check-off in the anthracite field.

The periodic discontent of anthracite miners with the leadership of John L. Lewis erupted in late 1941. The checked off dues were too high. The miners protested a fifty cent monthly increase in union dues which now reached $1.50 monthly, $18.00 per year. Of the monthly total, 90 cents went to the national office, 30 cents to the district and 30 cents to the local union. The local unions felt their treasuries were very inadequate, claiming they could not even pay expenses of members for a trip to Washington. In December, 1941, the local unions voted a walk-out. The national union under Lewis tried patriotic appeals to get the men back to work, the same appeals Lewis was later to ignore from President Harry Truman.

The national magazine, *Life*, carried two pictures of striking miners gathered at the corner of Brown and Parrish

124

Streets in Wilkes-Barre, and at the Huber Colliery union hall in Ashley. When the patriotic appeal of Lewis failed, President Roosevelt intervened and ordered the men back to work. The miners obeyed his order.

Lewis reacted vociferously when, unbelievably, the Office of Price Administration (O.P.A.) granted soft-coal operators a 23 cent per ton increase in prices. Lewis ripped into his foes. "When mine workers' children cry for bread, they cannot be satisfied with (wage) . . . formula (or) . . . anti-inflation dissertation." He asked for a $2.00 per day increase plus a package including safety rules and paid vacations. Lewis could not see operators being rewarded while miners were asked to live within limits.

No one believed Lewis would dare to strike during wartime, risking the furor of the public and the press. Some senators on the Truman Investigating Committee were intent on "showing up" Lewis so that he would not dare to strike. The committee looked into profits in war-time industry and asked Lewis to appear so that the nation would feel the committee was policing labor as well as capital.

The manner in which Lewis handled the antagonistic senators is both revealing of his personality and entertaining:

Senator Brewster: ". . . we hope the rich will not get richer."

Lewis: "We all hope . . . but hope deferred maketh a sick heart."

Senator Brewster: "If we waited for reasonable prices, Hitler would be at our shores."

Lewis: "Do you mean . . . American industry wouldn't provide essential war goods . . . unless guaranteed profits?"

Lewis also dropped this block-buster: "Congress can't condone a policy in this country that fattens industry and starves labor and then calls upon labor to starve patriotically."

The committee hearing became heated as Senators Ball and Brewster leaped at Lewis:

125

Senator Ball: "Mr. Lewis, you are not seriously (saying) that . . . workers are not getting enough to eat? That is demagoguery and you know it!"

Lewis (angrily): ". . . when you call me a demagogue before you give me a chance to reply, I'll hurl it back in your face, sir!"

Senator Truman: (You must not make any) "sassy remarks to the committee."

Lewis: "Who cast the first stone?"

Lewis continued defining hunger as the dietary deficiencies of laboring men working physically eight hours a day. Under cross-examination, he infuriated the committee by frequently answering "not necessarily."

One of the last exchanges between Senator Burton and Lewis reveals the Lewis touch.

Senator Burton: "If we restrain industry and finance, are you willing to work on holding down wages?"

Lewis: (sneering) "My dear Senator, whenever you have restrained industry and finance, just call me on the phone."

Lewis still threatened a war-time strike, an unheard of action. Critics as well as friends believed the Roosevelt administration was out to "get him." The operators stood by, hoping that Lewis realized his vulnerability, and tried to attain a settlement which included a revision of his demands on the operators. No contract came.

Finally, Lewis announced to the press that the strike that no one believed possible was on. Miners, 450,000 soft-coal miners, were ordered not to trespass on coal property without a contract. Furthermore, he called for the elimination of the government agencies, especially the War Labor Board, as go-betweens for capital and labor. He wanted collective bargaining restored and government protection for the operators removed. President Roosevelt wired Lewis ". . . as Commander-in-Chief, I will use all my power against your actions which in effect are as crippling as defeat in the field."

Lewis and the miners did not respond. The nation gawked, stood, unbelieving, open-mouthed, shocked. Headlines turned larger, blacker. War news disappeared. *The New York Times* headlined "Coal Mines Closing, Defying Roosevelt Order. President Ready to Seize Pits This Morning. Lewis Unshaken."

Lewis unshaken was the key. John L. Lewis was leading half a million miners in direct defiance of the Commander-in-Chief. It was revolution. Roosevelt seized the mines, put Secretary of the Interior Ickes in charge, made the operators employees of the government and ordered the miners back to work under the government.

All eyes turned to Lewis to see what his next move would be. While he made up his mind, his character was demolished at home and on the fields of battle. The Stars and Stripes damned his "coal black soul." A united front of every political persuasion—including the Communists, now behind the war effort—vied with epithets of traitor, saboteur, fascist.

Lewis evidently never considered his actions treasonous. He knew that the stockpile of coal in the United States was ample for months. He did not believe that the war effort was in danger, except in the press, on the radio, and in the minds of the government officials. Furthermore, he knew the casualties in the pits were tragic, too. He often compared, in an exaggerated way, the casualties of the miners with those of the soldiers. While the nation seethed and raged, he made an agreement with Secretary Ickes to go back to work for a two-week period until the "new employer" had time to "appraise . . . the problems." This announcement was made fifteen minutes before President Roosevelt was to go on national radio. The radio waves were filled with news of agreement. Roosevelt, annoyed by this upstaging, sat with two speeches before him, one soft and one hard. He chose the hard line, lambasting Lewis.

Roosevelt needed more authority but he was afraid of the

proposed Smith-Connally Act. Fearing to hurt his friends, he vetoed the Smith-Connally bill,[2] but Congress enacted it over his veto. The Smith-Connally Act became law. In the meantime, Lewis was successful in signing contracts with the operators who were enjoying the prosperity brought on by the war. The mines were not removed from unlimited government supervision, however, until a half-million hard and soft coal miners struck on November 1, 1943. Roosevelt was, at that time, compelled to agree to a contract between the government and the miners, an agreement which he had previously rejected with a resounding "no." The contract was attacked as a victory for Lewis. Economists said that the money gains were small profits in return for the antagonism of the American people.

When Truman became president after Roosevelt's death in 1945, he issued orders to fight Lewis, saying that the government must prevail. When Lewis attempted to disregard a government agreement, Clark Clifford, Counsel to Truman, and Tom Clark, Attorney General, obtained an injunction from Judge Goldsborough. Lewis fought the injunction, lost, and a fine of $3,500,000 was levied on the union, and a $10,000 fine on him personally. The Supreme Court upheld his guilt, but reduced the union's fine to $700,000. Lewis, the giant-killer, was mauled. Truman, the insignificant, emerged as a personality in his own right. More importantly, the government showed that it could compel a labor-management agreement. Lewis, in character, called Truman totally unfit for the presidency. Truman testily asserted that Lewis was unfit for the position of dog-catcher. In his private papers, published in 1980, Truman described John L. Lewis in more detail: "He is a Hitler at heart, a

---

[2] The Smith-Connally Act became law over the veto of President Roosevelt. The law gave the President the right to seize striking industries. It also declared strikes illegal in government controlled industry. Violations were punishable by fine and imprisonment.

demagogue in action and a traitor in fact. In 1942, he should have been hanged for treason."

In 1950, Lewis moved into his seventies, growing older and weaker. The coal industry, too, became weaker to the point that the anthracite industry neared death. The competition from oil and gas battered the bituminous areas as well. Most of the labor leaders who were contemporaries of Lewis died in office. Lewis must have planned to do the same. However, he did not, and before he died at the age of 80, he turned over the reins to his vice-president, Tom Kennedy, who was 73.

For half a century, John L. Lewis had been a United Mine Worker. For over thirty years, the colorful, quotable, preposterous Welsh egotist had been a leader, often progressive, but more often, opportunistic and self-centered. The anthracite workers could not describe it, but they felt somehow that their union and their leader were at once undemocratic and erratic, and though Lewis sometimes produced victories, he often failed them. Nevertheless, Lewis was their leader and the U. M. W. was their union.

John L. Lewis took his historic place with Terence Powderly and John Mitchell as the triumverate of anthracite mining unionization. These three figures led the coal crusade for labor justice. Their personalities shared similarities and differences. Terence Powderly, the railroader, was a philosophical man, a believer in temperance, a humanistic Catholic. John Mitchell, a miner at age 12, became a soft-spoken conciliator. John L. Lewis, also a miner as a teenager, was an aggressive bible-quoting, Shakespeare-spouting, wily infighter, and politically knowledgeable slugger. The three caught the spirit of America during the industrialization of the nation. All accepted capitalism; all wanted to purify it. To them capitalism exploiting labor was not a viable economic nor political system, yet not one of the three sympathized with socialism or communism. The three were anathema to Eugene Debs, Mother Jones and Big Bill Haywood. Typically and ironically, the three were maligned as capitalistic opportunists by the more radical left, while at the same time they were buffeted as socialists by conservatives.

The three men were typically American in their optimistic belief in progress and in their advocacy of education. All three were humanistic Christians. Working for the mining immigrants, they made the unbearable bearable. For the Welsh, the Irish, Polish, Lithuanian, Slovak, Italians and English, these three men were the great emancipators, despite their errors and inadequacies.

John L. Lewis, the scowling, formidable Welsh president of the United Mine Workers, once called "the most visible sight in the nation's capital, next to the Washington Monument," was seldom photographed with rank and file members as seen above.

Lewis, shown at left, celebrates John Mitchell Day at the statue of the U.M.W. hero, Court House Square, Scranton.

CHAPTER X

Anthracite Threat to All Mining People

Mining Subsidence

Even while John L. Lewis was locked in combat with F. D. R. during World War II, the anthracite mines continued to produce at levels unrealized since predepression days. In addition to the production from the old line companies, there was additional output from smaller companies sub-leasing coal properties from the major producers. As a result of the increased production and the activities of sub-lessors, Wyoming Valley suffered from a resurgence of an old problem: land subsidence caused by the mining of anthracite coal.

While miners and their families were the victims of explosions, escaping gas, falling roofs, and other mine fatalities, the general public, regardless of occupation or class, was the victim of land subsidence caused by the mining of anthracite. Land subsidence has been a pervasive problem in the life of Wyoming Valley since the Civil War. Even today, after expenditures of millions of dollars for backfilling, either hydraulically or pneumatically, the problem persists.

Subsidence in Wyoming Valley has been both exaggerated and underestimated. Its exaggeration has irritated those working to attract new industries, ordinarily a difficult task, an impossible one when the Valley is pictured as unstable and threatening. In order to minimize the problem, its reality has often been ignored and thus underestimated, often by the very people who would benefit most by its recognition and solution. No history of the influences impinging on the life of the people of Wyoming Valley would be complete without noting highlights of the complex problems.

When anthracite coal was mined, precautions had to be taken to allow enough coal to remain as pillars to support the roof of the mine and the surface above. In addition, artificial supports were built as reinforcements. Unfortunately, these precautions were often neglected, for anthracite coal, like most United States resources, was often mined as quickly and as cheaply as possible, with a view to low production costs and not to social welfare. As a result, unsupported coal and rock within the mine often shifted, sagged, or caved. This shifting of the earth caused a man-made, localized earthquake which had two catastrophic results: it destroyed land, homes, public buildings and human life on the surface and it destroyed thousands of tons of unmined coal, which deprived the nation of valuable reserves.

Subsidence is not exclusively a Pennsylvania problem. It has plagued most of the mining areas of the world. Disasters from subsidence have been noted in England, Wales, France, Germany, and Japan. Worldwide, much of the subsidence has occurred over underdeveloped and uninhabited land, and the social consequences were negligible. In northeastern Pennsylvania, however, the area is densely populated and the social and economic effects striking. The city-by-city, borough-by-borough accounts of subsidence reveal damages to homes, institutions, public and private buildings, roads, highways and undeveloped lands. The financial losses add up to millions of dollars. The losses and deprivations caused by subsidence, however, are minor by comparison to the tragedies suffered by some victims. Perhaps the most heart-rending was the death of Jule Ann Fulmer.[1]

About 1:30 p.m., the afternoon of February 8, 1944, Mrs. Marie Mitchell with her niece Jule Ann Fulmer, age 2, and her nephew, David Fulmer, age 5, were walking on Mill Street

---

[1] For a more detailed list of tragedies see *Subsidence Caused by the Mining of Anthracite Coal*, Roberts, Ellis W., Doctoral Dissertation, New York University, 1948.

in Pittston, returning from a grocery store. Mrs. Mitchell handed little Jule Ann an orange. The child released her aunt's hand, took the orange and momentarily lagged a few short steps behind. The aunt turned to look at the child, but the child had disappeared suddenly as the sidewalk and earth collapsed.

Mr. Thomas Hennigan, seated in his living room and hearing the screaming of the aunt and the commotion, ran outside, peered into the gaping hole, but could not see the child. He called the fire department and a ladder was put into the hole, which was only a few feet in diameter but over twenty feet deep. Firemen descended, but still could not find the child.

While hundreds of people gathered at the scene, it was decided to get a steam-shovel. A shovel and a bull-dozer arrived and began to dig into the earth for the child. Thirty hours later, after 550 tons of rock, coal, sand and dirt had been removed, a small hand appeared from the side of the excavation. Mine inspector Andrew Wilson of Hazleton, Joseph Gross of Duryea, and George Stoffer of Port Griffith descended to where the body lay. They carefully extricated it and brought it to the surface. The body lay about twenty feet below the surface. The steam shovel had dug to a depth of forty feet. As the child had fallen, she had been sucked into the side of the cave and her body had, therefore, remained unobserved by searchers for thirty hours.

With an oft-used expression popular during the war years, William Watson, Pittston correspondent for the *Times Leader Evening News*, stated "Little Jule Ann Fulmer, 2 years old, died yesterday in what should be the safest place in the world today—the streets of an American city."

There is no doubt that the citizens of Pittston were incensed. As crowds gathered on Mill Street to watch the rescue squads work to find and remove the body of the small child, it was not unusual to hear individuals rail against coal operators with "If that was my child I would kill the _____

134

with my own hands . . . if I 'hung' for it!" But this wild threat seldom developed into rational protest.

Again, reporter William Watson effectively warned of the failure to channel the flame of indignation into constructive activity. Having witnessed many subsidence tragedies and having observed the apathy of the people many times, he wrote with earnest sincerity:

> Today officials of Pittston are incensed. The State Legislature is incensed or should be. A feeling of anger swept over every American who read . . . (of) Jule Ann Fulmer . . . The residents . . . are in a determined mood to put a halt to further disaster by demanding immediate action. PERHAPS the same thing occurred . . . when 150 homes on Railroad Street were wrecked by mine caves. It was 'all out for victory' . . . yet nothing of consequence was ever accomplished. Why?
>
> Perhaps this tragedy will result in welding a united front in Pittston to fight the mine cave threat. Pehaps little Jule Ann Fulmer will be the unwitting martyr for Pittston's future. PERHAPS.

To understand the "Why?" and "Perhaps" in the editorial, it is necessary to look at the law. It is futile to rail against the apathy of the people if the avenues of reform and correction are already closed. The principle that an owner or lessee of subjacent stratum must support higher strata and the surface above it had been established in English and American courts. Questions of reckless mining, the nature of the land, difficulties in providing the support, the comparative cost of the surface and minerals are immaterial and did not modify the principle. The right of support could not be qualified by evasive or implied statements. The right of surface support could only be negated by strongly expressed and precise language. The last sentence accounts for language found in almost every property deed in the anthracite area, language that conveys only surface rights and excludes mineral rights.

A look at the law and its interpretation by the courts

reveals the reasons why subsidence problems persisted. The most important single case was Mahon v. Pennsylvania Coal Company. The case tested the constitutionality of the Pennsylvania Kohler-Fowler Law, an act making mining which causes subsidence a criminal offense.

The case began late in 1921 when Harold J. Mahon and his wife, Margaret Craig Mahon, attempted to obtain an injunction against the Pennsylvania Coal Company to restrain the company from mining so as to injure their property. The surface land, or property involved, had been inherited by Mrs. Margaret Craig Mahon from her father, Alexander Craig. The mineral or mining rights had been sold in 1878 by Alexander Craig to the Pennsylvania Coal Company. The deed was explicit in removing the liability of the coal corporation for any surface damage done while mining. However, the Mahons proceeded to ask for the injunction because the Kohler-Fowler Act, passed by the Pennsylvania legislature, was equally as explicit in stating that, regardless of expressed stipulations freeing coal companies from liability, a coal company mining so as to cause subsidence was committing a criminal act.

The Luzerne County Court, once with Judge Fuller presiding, and again sitting as the court en banc,[2] refused to grant the injunction. The case was then taken to the State Supreme Court.

The State Supreme Court reversed the opinion of Judge Fuller, dismissing a bill in equity for an injunction. The opinion of the State Supreme Court was written by Judge C. J. Moschzisker. Judge Moschzisker's opinion was the highest legal expression holding that the Kohler-Fowler Act of 1921 was constitutional. Pointing out that the anthracite industry had endangered property and life for many years, Judge Moschzisker held that, in order to serve the public welfare, the state,

---

[2] Court en banc. Court session with all judges sitting and hearing evidence.

through its police power, may restrict the use of private property because all property is held under the obligation to use it so as not to injure the public. This protection, according to the court, extended to homeowners even when contracts or deeds contained expressed words absolving the subsurface owner from liability. The court described the historical and external conditions in the anthracite area which necessitated the legislation. Considering the state of affairs, the court deemed the legislature authorized to remedy these conditions.

Other sections of Judge Moschzisker's ruling held that: It is not necessary to depend upon the owner of the property or his special interest to move against persons causing subsidence. Action may be initiated to protect the whole community. The classification of lands to be safeguarded against subsidence is not arbitrary, but proper, and the separation of anthracite from bituminous regions is sound. Finally, he reiterated and maintained that the state's use of police power shall not be held unconstitutional because it interferes with the use of private property.

Justice Kephart wrote a lengthy dissenting opinion. His summary is quoted here at length because its reasoning was adopted by the Supreme Court of the United States and served to kill the Kohler-Fowler Act. It was this decision which ultimately led to the continuing chaotic conditions in the anthracite area.

> It is entirely unnecessary, in order to protect life, to forbid mining of coal. A notice such as I have suggested would fully protect all except those who, being of full age and sound mind, voluntarily go where it is not safe for them to be.
>
> The provisions of the Fowler Act clearly show that this is merely part of a scheme to force the coal companies to support the surface of owners who have either for value released the right of support or have purchased their lots for a less price by reason of not acquiring this right with their purchase.
>
> I can conceive of no reason—if it be necessary for the public good that the surface be supported—why, as in the case of the rent laws, fair compensation should not be provided, save

only the desire of the beneficiaries to get something for nothing.

The entire purpose and design of this legislation (Fowler-Kohler Act), is clearly, to my mind, to force the coal companies, who have already paid for this property once, to pay for it again, and to give to the surface owners a valuable right for which they have already been paid.

The Pennsylvania Coal Company, having lost its case in the Pennsylvania Supreme Court, decided to appeal the case, and the dispute made its way to the highest court in the United States. The Supreme Court ruled in favor of the coal company. In reversing the Pennsylvania Supreme Court, the United States Supreme Court invalidated the Kohler-Fowler Act and freed the coal corporations from this legislative control. This decision has impeded most efforts to establish responsibility and liability for subsidence caused by the mining of anthracite coal.

The most shocking aspect of the Supreme Court decision is that the majority decision was written by the great liberal Justice Oliver Wendell Holmes. As Mr. Max Lerner pointed out in a brief reference to the case, it is unusual to read Holmes stating, "We are in danger of forgetting that a strong public desire to improve the public condition is not enough to warrant achieving the desire by a shorter cut than the constitutional way of paying for the change." There seemed to be little need, if any, to utter this precaution to his fellow members on the court. It is equally as disturbing to read Holmes remarking, "A source of damage to such a house is not a public nuisance, even if similar damage is inflicted on others in different places."

These statements of Holmes, along with the following, became the principles upon which anti-cavein legislation was defeated in Pennsylvania for the next twenty-five years. Holmes added that:

1. The Fowler-Kohler Act was not a legitimate exercise of police power.

2. If regulation goes too far, it shall be tantamount to expropriation.

3. Property owners are shortsighted if they obtain only surface rights to their property and not mineral rights also.

4. The right to coal consists in the right to mine that coal.

5. A restriction on mining is not justified as protection of personal safety, since personal safety could be provided for by notice from the coal company.

6. There was not reciprocity in the proposed regulation by law. The coal companies would not benefit. All the benefits would accrue to one group to the disadvantage of the other.

7. The damage is not common or public.

Justice Brandeis, a liberal voice on the Supreme Court, differed sharply with Holmes and wrote the dissenting opinion. His views in this case represent a concern for the public welfare consistent with his whole legal philosophy. Brandeis' principal contentions in the case were as follows: The rights of an owner, as against the public, are not increased by dividing the interest in his property into surface and sub-soil. He said, "The value of the coal kept in place by the restriction may be negligible as compared with the value of the whole property." Brandeis also contended that if railroads could be compelled to build grade crossings to protect the public even when they had contracts to the contrary, and if a railroad could be held liable for the death of employees even when they had a charter exempting them, then the state of Pennsylvania could take measures to protect the safety of all by restricting mining even though companies had legal rights to mine. Brandeis argued further that "One whose rights . . . are subject to state restrictions, cannot remove them from the power of the state by making a contract about them." Here he was specifically stating that, regardless of the deal which the Pennsylvania Coal Company had received from Alexander Craig absolving the corporation from subsidence liability, the coal company was still subject to state restriction or law which was, in this case, the Kohler-Fowler Act.

In vehement disagreement with the charge that only individuals or private persons were involved, Justice Brandeis stated the theory that, "Protecting the community through invoking the aid as litigant of interested private citizens is not a novelty in our law." Brandeis admitted that the case involved only a private dwelling, but he called attention to the fact that the Kohler-Fowler Act dealt with subsidence of public buildings, churches, schools, hospitals, theaters, halls, railroads, etc. Therefore, he held that it was obvious that the law was passed for a public purpose. In conclusion, he called attention to any number of owners who were prohibited from operating oil tanks, brickyards, livery stables, billiard halls, oleomargarine factories, and breweries when the operation of these industries adversely affected the public.

The 5–4 decision left the coal companies free to mine with impunity, except where homes and public buildings were covered by deeds containing sub-surface rights. In the Wyoming Valley, few such deeds existed.

There is some evidence indicating that the Pennsylvania v. Mahon case was not a heated controversy between subsidence victims and a coal corporation, but rather a test case initiated by the Pennsylvania Coal Company, with the wealthy Mahon family, itself a holder of coal interests, as the Pennsylvania Coal Company's friendly "opponent."

Damage and threats to property and life from land subsidence over formerly mined areas still are common. Despite millions of dollars spent in back-filling old voids, there still remains under the Wyoming Valley a complex maze of mining roadways, tunnels, gangways and breasts. But chaotic conditions underground caused by flooding and caving make the remaining coal virtually inaccessible; with these conditions, caving will continue.

The most recent trauma occurred in the summer of 1982 when Gerald White was killed in a subsidence in Scranton.

Ironically, White was killed while in the process of back-filling in an area which collapsed and claimed his life. White was an employee of Empire Construction Company, working under a federal contract to fill an abandoned mine shaft on Capouse Avenue in Scranton.

Some mining engineers contend that the millions of gallons of water in the mines, a result of natural accumulations and the Knox Mine Disaster, is actually a positive support. Without this water, they say, caving would indeed be even more catastrophic.

Fortunately, today, property owners may now purchase subsidence insurance. This insurance became available as a result of citizen activity and involvement. In the 1950's, a group spearheaded by the Reverend Edmund John of Forty Fort pushed a bill to successful enactment. It was not easy. The first attempt at passage was vetoed by Governor Lawrence. Another attempt followed a year later. After a personal conference with the governor, a delegation from the Wyoming Valley citizens' group convinced him of the merits of the bill and gained his support. The law was enacted in 1962.

The subsidence insurance and continual back-filling are forms of relief available. In the Spring of 1983, several subsidence cases revealed that the problem of land subsidence caused by the mining of anthracite coal is a continuing one. Federally financed back-filling has helped to stabilize the surface area, as have the natural conditions described above. Nevertheless, periodically, some land subsidence headlines the media news. Fortunately new industrial and commercial companies attracted to the Wyoming Valley can still find acres of stable and attractive land unthreatened by land subsidence. The Back Mountain, Mountain Top, and Crestwood Park areas have been unaffected.

However, land subsidence in the anthracite region remains a threat to life and property. The persistence of subsidence aggravates the dangers from abandoned shafts, slopes, mine voids, and abandoned stripping pits, and accents, too, their hazardous presence in northeastern Pennsylvania.

The dangers from mining were not only underground. Mine subsidence was a threat to all who lived in Pennsylvania's anthracite region. Mine cave-ins damaged or destroyed homes, schools, highways, and public buildings.

CHAPTER XI

The End of Anthracite in Wyoming Valley

The Knox Disaster, 1959

Much is written today about coal as a future energy source. But, in northeastern Pennsylvania, where once was mined 99 percent of the nation's anthracite, there is great skepticism about recovering the estimated fifteen billion tons of coal still underground. The mines of the northern anthracite district, which once warmed the homes and mansions of Boston, Philadelphia, and New York are now flooded or caved. To understand the problem in the Wilkes-Barre area of the Wyoming Valley, one must turn to January, 1959, and the Knox Mine Disaster.

Accidents in the anthracite area at Avondale in Plymouth in 1869, at Twin Shaft in Pittston in 1896, and at the Baltimore Tunnel in Wilkes-Barre in 1919 were costly in terms of lives and property. But there was always recovery. Disasters were generally localized, so that at some point the fires, the cave-ins, and the escaping gases were controlled. Mining went on even though many lives did not. This was not so after the Knox Disaster.

The ailing anthracite industry in Wyoming Valley began its final death struggle on January 22, 1959. On that day, the whole industry in Wyoming Valley was devastated as a result of greed, and error, and the rampaging, ice-filled Susquehanna River which poured into the hole created by reckless mining. Ironically, January 22, 1890 was the date of the founding of the United Mine Workers. The total devastation

143

of the Knox Disaster was not immediately apparent. The immensity and totality of the destruction was not known for many days. But the devastation, coming sixty-nine years to the day after the founding of the United Mine Workers, wiped out the anthracite industry in the Wyoming Valley.

The Knox Mine Disaster is a story—of a river, a mine, and the men who worked in that mine. The story begins with the Susquehanna River. Watered by the Chemung in New York, it flows south from the Pennsylvania-New York border through brilliant scenic valleys and mountains, passing the beautiful Indian-named towns of Towanda, Wyalusing, Meshoppen, Mehoopany, Tunkhannock, and others. Flowing south, the Susquehanna is sheltered on the north side by Appalachian Ranges, called the Endless Mountains. On its right bank, there is a profusion of valleys, some cultivated and farmed, others used as grazing pastures for dairy herds. The Susquehanna, in this pastoral setting, appears to be a peaceful stream, but naturalists proclaim it a fast-moving body of water. Moreover, it is a fast-rising river, as cities downstream can attest. In 1972, when the waters gathered by Hurricane Agnes poured into the Susquehanna River from its surrounding valleys and mountains, the river bulged into a gigantic force, flooding the farms, towns, and cities on its banks in the costliest natural disaster in American history.

In 1959, the river was not as high and rapid as it was later in 1972 but it was rising from a January thaw. It was almost sixteen feet, filled with ice, and rising. As the ice-filled river flowed through Pittston, West Pittston and Port Griffith, it passed a number of shafts, slopes and airways owned by the Pennsylvania Coal Company, but leased to small independent operators.

One of these relatively small mines was being leased to a company called the Knox Coal Company. The mine was in Port Griffith, a small community just south of the city of Pittston. Most of these mine entrances were not visible to passing motorists, but they were there. Within the mine lay the Pittston vein, one of the richest beds of coal in the area. The vein running eight to ten feet in thickness was a rich, pure, black vein of the finest anthracite. Unfortunately the rich vein ran precariously close to the river bed so that state mine inspectors had red-lined a point on the mine maps beyond which mining was prohibited. Reputable mining dictates caution in such areas, not only for safety of the miners but also for the protection of the coal property and the company's investment.

The temptation to mine for profit by the extraction of the rich coal was too great. As the coal was removed beneath the bed of the Susquehanna River, the barrier supporting the mine roof was weakened by the pressure of the high, raging, ice-filled river. The swollen river smashed into the mines in a raging torrent of water and ice.

On January 22, 1959, when the river broke through, eighty-seven men were working underground in the Knox Mine. The men were scattered throughout the mine workings. One group of eleven men was under the supervision of Frank Hanley of Plymouth. Hanley saw water swirling before him. Luckily, he was close to the front of the shaft, near the cage. Calling the eleven, he led them to the shaft and rang for the cage. As the cage began to rise, the water had reached hip level. After interminable minutes, the cage reached the surface and these men were clear, above ground, and free.

The men who got out with Frank Hanley quickly spread the alarm. Immediately radio and television spread the news. The afternoon newspaper, *The Times Leader*, headlined: Three Dead; Forty Trapped. The hurried headline was not quite accurate, but it reflected the seriousness of the tragedy.

Relatives, friends, neighbors, and curiosity-seekers rushed to the scene. As they stood on the high rock ledge in Port Griffith, they looked down on the double tracks of the Lehigh Valley Railroad. There lapping at the tracks, was the rapidly-rising, ice-filled Susquehanna River. Just beyond they saw

145

an amazing site. There, a turbulent whirlpool told them that the ice-filled Susquehanna was pouring into the Knox Mine. The fate of those trapped was uncertain. Their rescue depended on stopping or slowing the rushing river, by somehow plugging the gaping hole. But the cavernous opening and the swirling waters presented insurmountable problems. The turbulent whirlpool swallowed dirt and fill like a ravenous beast.

As officials viewed the destructive force of the swirling maelstrom, the immensity of the tragedy drove them to desperate action. It was obvious that if the river could not be controlled, not only were the lives of the entombed men at stake, but also the life of the whole anthracite industry in Wyoming Valley, since most of the underground mines were interconnected by drainage tunnels. There were few barriers to halt the surging waters from running mine to mine throughout the whole valley.

Since the Lehigh Valley Railroad tracks paralleled the river and came to a point just above the swirling waters, a dramatic decision was made. Officials felt that a few of the large coal gondolas dropped into the whirlpool might plug it at the point where the original break-through had occurred. Lehigh Valley Railroad crews cut the rails and pointed the track toward the river. A yard engine pushed the huge coal cars as close as safety allowed and let them roll under their own power off the end of the tacks into the swirling river below. As cars were pushed and rolled into the cavernous opening, they disappeared with a slurp like toys into a sewer line.

Opposite the river, on the side of the Lehigh Valley tracks, close enough to be touched by trainmen, another perpendicular ledge of rock rises straight up about one hundred feet to the street level of Port Griffith. From high above at this point, hundreds of smaller coal cars were also dumped over the cliff into the raging river hole. Closing the gigantic break-in proved too much for the brain and brawn of the supervisors and their workers. Thousands of tons of equipment and debris were ineffective. They worked frantically to close the enormous break-in, even though they knew the men still in the mine could hardly escape the raging waters. Occupied with the gargantuan river problem, they had no way of knowing how the mine workers were faring. Were they drowned in the first rush of water or had they in some way escaped the raging flood?

Inside the mine, other men were defending themselves against the rampaging river in another way. Among them and responsible for many of the mine workers was Myron Thomas, an assistant foreman of the Knox Coal Company. The day had started routinely for Myron Thomas. On the morning of January 22, 1959, he had accompanied Joseph Stella inspecting work being done. Stella was an employee of the Pennsylvania Coal Company, the lessor of the Knox Mine. Periodically he would enter the mine to check and verify that the leasing company, the Knox, was complying with permits granted to it. About noon, while Thomas had a sandwich, Stella stood by waiting for him. They planned to walk together to the Marcy Vein hoist. Thomas, relating the events of the day stated, "While eating I heard my haulage motor speeding toward us. Getting up, I went to inquire about the motor's excessive speed. The motorman yelled to me to get all my men outside fast.

"I instructed him to continue on and to contact all my men. I told him not to forget four company men who were cleaning and propping up an old chamber, to have every man wait for me at the Marcy Hoist and not leave there until I arrived.

"Joe Stella and I continued there . . . and found a few men waiting. At this point you could hear a roar of water pouring in from a point out closer to the May Shaft section which I knew was a lower elevation." Thomas, descending

147

to the Marcy Slope, saw the motorman again and received his assurance that all men had been notified. When the men did not appear, Thomas left to go for them.

"I saw them coming at a slow pace. I yelled to them to hurry up because the water was gushing in, and they started to run." Finding that the water was moving toward the men at the head of the slope, his impulse was to join with Stella in leading the 32 men back under the river to the Schooley Shaft in Exeter. With the water flowing in rapidly and the men extremely perturbed, they turned instead through a rock tunnel to the Pittston Vein.

"My objective was to stay on the upper side of our old Pittston Vein pitch places and to try to get out the River Slope exit. At the time we did not know where the water broke through. After about 45 minutes of going through water, knocking down brattices in cross-cuts, so that we could stay on a higher elevation, we found the noise of the water terrific—just like a 60 mile an hour train boring down toward us. At this time, we knew walls were being pushed out, and huge blocks of ice and all sorts of debris were being pushed down the River Slope. We came to a blind chamber. A crosscut was full of water. The scene sent a shiver through us."

The group decided to retrace steps to get back to the Pittston Vein. "The men turned to the suggested direction, the younger ones running ahead. The older men were falling back.

"I yelled and yelled," said Thomas, "but I could not be heard because of the noise of the water which was deafening. I ran ahead till I caught up with the leaders. I told them it wasn't speed we needed but caution and prayer. I warned them of falling and fracturing a limb or spraining an ankle. I told them we would have to leave anyone injured and to try to get back with a rescue crew."

Again they tried the Marcy Vein. There was no water pouring down, but, fearing that the water was impeded by

148

a jam of debris and ice, and that if the jam were dislodged, the water would engulf them, they moved on searching for the Eagle Shaft.

After six hours, near collapse and total exhaustion, they had reached a dry area, free of water, and spacious enough for the group to spread out and rest. To their dismay, they realized they had lost one leader, Stella, and five other men. Where had they gone?

Stella, in the meantime, had chosen to move more slowly in order to stay with a handful of the older men who were unable to keep up with the others. Somehow, instinctively, he and the five older men with him, now separated from the other men, had made a turn when they "felt a flow of fresh air." They followed the airflow and realized that they had stumbled across an opening to the surface. An abandoned shaft had been left open for air. The air shaft was a perpendicular opening, seemingly impossible to climb because it had no ledges. But one of the group, Amedeo Pancotti, climbed it, literally by his finger nails and shoe-tips, an unbelievable, impossible climb out of the mine, which ultimately led to the rescue of his fellow workers. For this feat, Amedeo Pancotti was later awarded the Carnegie Medal.

Amedeo, whose command of English was very limited, minimized his heroism. He related with humor what had happened after he had safely reached the surface. The opening through which he had escaped was along the Lehigh Valley Railroad tracks, a few hundred yards from the area where a frenzied army of workers was trying to plug the river opening. After reaching the top of the air shaft on the surface, he stumbled down the tracks and approached one of the company officials, superintendent Robert Groves. It was a dark, winter-twilight hour. The superintendent disregarded Amedeo, thinking that he was one of the many men working on the recovery project. Finally, in very broken English, Amedeo somehow got the full attention of Groves. Mr. Groves turned, eyed Amedeo inquisitively and asked, "What hole?

149

You keep pointing to a hole. What hole?" Exasperated and exhausted, Amedeo Pancotti finally made it known that Stella and his small group were at the bottom of the air shaft awaiting rescue.

A flurry of frantic activity produced quick results. Ropes were dropped down the air hole, and Stella and the other four companions of Amedeo were pulled to the surface, weary and frightened after their long hours of groping through darkness in waist-high cold, Susquehanna River water.

There were still men lost in the mine. Myron Thomas and his men, now numbering 25, moved from the working chamber through old unfamiliar passages. To preserve lights, Thomas ordered every other man to extinguish his light. The line of men plodded and crawled mile after mile, as one of them said later, "like chipmunks under the ground." There was little conversation. As the hours went by, the desperate, quiet, frightened men, in a single line, stumbled, crawled, and dragged themselves through pitch-dark caverns, very dimly lit by the few burning headlamps. They knew that any moment the water might over-take them. They knew, too, that the old mine workings, supported only by rotting timbers, unattended for years, could cave in and trap them where they were. Recalling the excruciating experience, Thomas describes his thoughts in the threatening blackness and near imminent death desperately searching for Eagle Shaft. "I did not tell them that I did not know exactly how to get there, that I knew only the general direction." He asked the men to pray, "to ask the Lord to show us the way out."

Walking through the old passages filled with rubble and coal was treacherous. The search for the exit led them to many old dead-end working areas. Thomas describes the frustrated search. "Now I was mixed up in my direction. My only hope was to find my last working place, but I could not find it. I had chalked my way, not knowing that other men

150

were marking their way. Some of the men would run up a chamber, marking it, others down another. In the end the whole area was marked. We came to a place where water was gushing down. We thought we could get through holding on an abandoned power line. But the water rose to our stomachs and hit us with such force that we had to abandon that way. Retracing our steps we again reached a higher elevation. It was now about six o'clock. Our lights were growing dim. Our nerves were now at razor's edge."

After nearly another hour of desperate exploration in dead-end chambers and old workings, they came to a badly-rotted wooden door with several barely discernible letters—E-g--Shaft. The disintegrating door was broken easily and a gust of air streamed into the small opening. But what was once a passageway was blocked by massive caving. An argument ensued. Some of the men agreed to crawl through the small opening. Others wanted to retreat fearing they would be trapped beyond the opening. Myron Thomas, reminding them of the water below and the in-rushing air, convinced them to crawl through. It was the right decision. On the other side of the opening they saw lights and heard voices.

It was now seven o'clock. After seven hours of searching, walking, stumbling, many times in waist-high, icy water, the men emerged from the claustrophobic blackness.

Myron Thomas described the last minutes of the ordeal. "We arrived at the foot of the Eagle Shaft. Watching each man have the rope placed on him and being hoisted up and hearing the outside words of happy greeting made me feel good. It was now my turn. Looking back into the blackness from where we escaped, I thanked God for showing me the way and thanked the men who years ago sunk the old Eagle Air Shaft."

As the last twenty-five men were pulled to the surface with rescue equipment, wet, exhausted, bruised, they were covered with blankets and rushed to nearby Pittston Hospital.

151

With the exception of twelve miners, every other man working in the Knox mine at the time of the break-through was saved.

Twelve men, who had evidently been working near the area where the river broke through, or who had tried different escape routes, were never found. Their bodies were never recovered. They were: Dominic Dovalesky, William Sinclair and Francis Bruno of Pittston; Frank Orloski of Dupont; John Bologa of Port Griffith; Dan Stefanaitis of Swoyersville; Herman Zalonis of Pittston Township; Sam Altieri of Hughestown; Benjamin Boyer of Forty Fort; Joseph Gezenski of Hunlock Creek; Eugene Ostroski of Wanamie; Charles Featherman of Muhlenberg.

The Pennsylvania General Assembly created a legislative committee to investigate the disaster. The committee was composed of State Representatives Laurence V. Gibb, James J. Jump, Stanley A. Meholchick, James Musto, William J. Reidenbach, and State Senators Harold E. Flack, Frank Kopriver, Jr., Paul Mahady, Martin L. Murray and Paul L. Wagner. The investigation uncovered numerous violations of state mining laws including an absence of professional engineering, planning, and supervision. Considerable neglect marked the whole mine operation.

The rock cover between the river and the mine had been set at 50 feet, but later reduced to 35 feet. The hearings established that the rock cover in some areas was only 19 inches.

Many of the workers testified that they were compelled to wear raincoats day after day. Because of the shallow rock cover, the seepage penetrated the mines and soaked the men. Evidently the lure of the rich Pittston vein was too seductive. The vein, eight to ten feet thick, was pure black, shining coal. Black diamonds were hard to resist.

The committee summarized its conclusions about the responsibility and causes of the disaster: 1) indifference of the Pennsylvania Coal Company, lessor, to general rules of safe mining; 2) the shortcuts used by the Knox Coal Company in its administrative and supevisory systems; 3) the evidence that the initiative pay system for the workers seduced them into ignoring their own safety; 4) the lack of design for mining, or for checking the mining, by professional mining engineers.

After hearing more than a thousand pages of testimony from owners, officials, and workers themselves, and after an evaluation of the causes, the committee made several recommendations. The most significant included: the appointment of at least one professional mining engineer to serve each of the anthracite districts. The engineer would approve all plans and permits for "under-water" mining, and assist mine inspectors. He also would evaluate the mine inspector's reports, inspect each mine once a year, and submit a report to the Secretary of Mines with his safety recommendations.

The committee recommended increased use of safety committees, improvements in the preparation and dissemination of reports and maps, a more complete and thorough knowledge of mine openings, and the posting of such information to preclude the "lost" experience of the Knox miners.

Recommended also were more severe penalties for mine law violations. The most severe penalty under the law was a misdemeanor fine of $500.00 or ninety days in jail or both. A mine operator violating a stop order issued by an inspector was liable only to pay a $50.00 fine or ten days in jail. The violations leading to the Knox disaster were punishable by a $50.00 fine. The legislative committee recommended the misdemeanor become a felony, punishable by a $5,000.00 fine and/or imprisonment in a penitentiary for not more than three years.

The Knox disaster revealed that after 100 years of mining in Northeastern Pennsylvania, the laws governing the safety of miners were abominably inadequate. The legislative committee itself referred to the laws as "archaic." However, the committee made no reference to the responsibility of the

Pennsylvania General Assembly for the laws. Legislative bodies usually write laws in a reflex action, reacting instead of anticipating needs. Visionary legislators are stymied by official apathy, special interests, or corporate objectives. Legislation designed to correct a potential threat, whether it be one of environment, highway safety, air traffic control, or public welfare is usually ignored until some tragedy erupts.

The devastating cost of the Knox disaster to the community can never be accurately assessed, but we know that twelve men lost their lives, a $1,000,000 payroll was lost, 3,000 men became unemployed, and, to all intents and purposes, deep-mining in Wyoming Valley ended. The Susquehanna River and the natural accumulation of earth and water filled the vast mine-workings under Wyoming Valley. The cost of the attempts to plug the river, of building a cofferdam and of sealing the hole with concrete was over three million dollars.

The cavernous gap was not filled until ten days after the break-through. When the hole was closed, workmen had to break through 30 feet of ice to get to the water in the mine. Eight men dropped a pump into the water. It began pumping out the water, which had rushed in at the rate of 12,123,000 gallons per minute. The water was ejected at the rate of 5,000 gallons a minute. The total amount of water to be pumped out was estimated at 40,000,000 gallons.

District Attorney Albert Aston and his assistant, Arthur Silverblatt, moved with dispatch after the tragedy to obtain the records of the Knox Coal Company. According to Stephen Teller who succeeded Albert Aston as district attorney, these records led to indictments and provided much of the evidence for the legal action that followed.

Coincidentally, Stephen Teller, the Luzerne County district attorney and prosecutor in two trials, one in Wilkes-Barre and the other in Easton because of a change of venue, is a sixth generation descendant of Judge Jesse Fell. Judge Jesse Fell was the first person to demonstrate the possibilities

154

of using anthracite coal as a domestic fuel. His success in burning coal in an open grate might be construed as the beginning of the Anthracite Era. His sixth generation descendant was present at its ending.

Reviewing conditions prevalent in mining prior to the disaster, courts found unbelievable arrangements prevailing. There was no valid labor-management relationship, just a "sweetheart" contract. A Federal Grand Jury found owners and officials of the United Mine Workers guilty of signing "sweetheart contracts," of paying and receiving money for "keeping labor peace." Two trials produced some justice, but the losses in human life, coal resources and a whole industry—the anthracite industry in Wyoming Valley—defy calculation.

On January 22, 1959, the swollen Susquehanna River broke into the Knox Colliery ending the Anthracite era in the Wyoming Valley.

Huge coal gondolas pushed into the turbulent, ice-filled Susquehanna River could not close the cavernous opening into the mine. The cars disappeared with a slurp, "like toys into a sewer line."

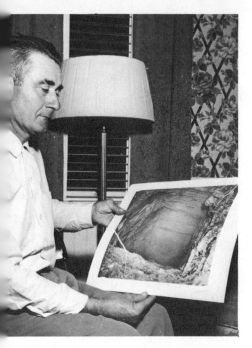

Amedeo Pancotti views the perpendicular walls of the Eagle Shaft which he climbed by his "fingernails and shoe tips." Pancotti's feat resulted in the rescue of a group of his fellow miners and earned him the Carnegie Medal.

Myron Thomas, an assistant foreman, led the last 25 men in the Knox Mine to safety. Escaping from the raging Susquehanna, Thomas and the men stumbled, crawled, and half-swam through the dark caverns before escaping by way of Eagle Shaft.

After seven horrifying hours, Joseph Soltis was pulled to safety along with the last men led by Myron Thomas, an assistant foreman at the colliery.

CHAPTER XII

The Heritage of Ethnic Miners

Epilogue

About a quarter of a century has passed since the Knox
disaster which to all intents marked the end of the anthracite
deep mining era. Were it not for an anniversary Mass said
each year on January 22 at St. Joseph's Church in Port Griffith, the event might be completely forgotten. The Masses
started by the Reverend Walter Sturski are still attended by
the families of victims and even some of the survivors of the
Knox disaster. On Sunday, January 23, 1982, on the grounds
of St. Joseph's Church in Port Griffith, a monument was
dedicated to the twelve victims. Twenty-four years after the
tragedy a small group of 100 or fewer people stood in the
cold rain under black umbrellas to hear again a prayer for
the lost twelve men.

Across the street from St. Joseph's Church, as one stands
on the high ledge near the Pittston Hospital and looks down
the Susquehanna River, one can see in the foreground, almost at his feet, the site of the Knox disaster. On the same
higher ground, on a clear day, one might squint and imagine
that he or she can see Holy Savior Church in the East End
of Wilkes-Barre, where Father Curran preached and de-
fended John Mitchell. Looking to the southwest, one might
see in the mind's eye, less than ten miles away, the moun-
tainside where the Avondale Breaker stood, the spot where
Terence Powderly was inspired at his Damascus. Looking
north, one might visualize the Twin Shaft in Pittston where
58 entombed men lie in their underground mine graves.

But most of all, when looking up and down the east and

158

west sides of the Susquehanna River, one may actually view the towns and boroughs where lived plain, heroic people. They were people who came from Wales, Ireland, England, Scotland, Poland, Lithuania, Russia, Italy, Czechoslovakia, and Yugoslavia. They came by boat, were challenged at Ellis Island, and then made their way to the Wyoming Valley. They believed in God and supported churches. They believed in education and encouraged their children. For as long as they could, they held on to their language and customs.

Finally, and most importantly, these men and women believed in the promise that was America. That promise was interpreted by Terence Powderly, John Mitchell, and John L. Lewis. These people lived through the tragedies of Avondale and the Twin Shaft, through the guns of Lattimer and the explosion at the Baltimore Colliery. They lived through disasters and depressions, labor conflicts and injustices. And they survived.

Today, in a corner of America, in northeastern Pennsylvania, the anthracite region is enhanced by the memory of these miners, their wives, and their children. They struggled to make a living, a living which in most cases was inextricably tied up with the mining of anthracite coal. Though many would have preferred it otherwise, their lives and fortunes were demeaned and, only occasionally, enhanced by the prosperity of the coal industry.

Today, as the sons and daughters, grandsons and granddaughters of these great people ponder their past and their roots, it is with gratitude and sometimes, if not always, with the hope and courage of their forebears. The descendants of these immigrant miners have roots of courage, humility and integrity.

159

Proper names of immigrant miners were often purposely shortened by mine timekeepers and sometimes inadvertently misspelled. The names listed here may not be the correct spelling.

AVONDALE DISASTER FATALITIES
September 6, 1869

Palmer Steele
Denison Slocum
John Bowen
William Powell
David Jones
Thomas Williams
William Williams (14 years old)
Willie Phillips
William Evans
Murray Edwards
Peter Conlin
Jacob Mosier
John Clark
William J. Evans
George Stackhouse
Edwin Jones
Morgan Watkins
Andrew Frothingham
William Allen
Thomas D. Jones
Peter Johnson
Evan Hughes
William Bowen
James Powell
Thomas Hughes
William Reese
William Porfit
William N. Williams
William Lewis
John Hughes
Thomas Morris
Elijah Bryant
Thomas Roberts
William Sink
Daniel Jones

David Thomas
Daniel Givens (17 years old)
Evan Rees
Edward W. Edwards
Henry Morris
William T. Williams
David S. Reese
Richard Woolley
John R. David
David James
William Williams
William Evans
Richard Owens
Willie Hatton (10 years old)
William Evans
James Powell
Thomas Hatton
Edward Owen
John Burtch
John Burtch, Jr. (12 years old)
John Jenkins
William R. Evans
Daniel Wood
William Nors (14 years old)
David Reese, Jr.
Griffith Roberts
John Ruth
Joseph Morris
Patrick McGurick
Henry Smith
Shem Howells
Thomas Davis
William Dewdle
John Roberts
Thomas Ryan

160

Hugh Gilroy
John Mahar
Patrick Burke
William T. Morgan
James Murray
Michael Daly
D. P. Pryer
James Phillips
James Williams
John D. Evans
William Harding
Samuel R. Morgan
William R. Evans
William Wildrich
Reese Lunday
Thomas Llewellyn
Reese Llewellyn
William David
John Thomas
John Davis

William T. Williams
William D. Johns
Darrius Guyter
William Rees
William Spick
John Harris
Thomas Jones
Thomas Phillips
Lewis David
Charles Fear
John Thomas
Dave Johnson
James Mallen
James Haskins
William D. Jones
Edward Taylor
Rowland Jones
Madison Alibach
Daniel Edwards
John Powell

DEATH LIST, TWIN SHAFT, PITTSTON
June 28, 1896

M. J. Langan
M. T. Lynott
Alex McCormack
Thomas Tenpenny
Michael Hughes
Cornelius McGuire
John Gill
Thomas O'Brien
Thomas Carden
John O'Boyle
James Golden
James McDonald
Edward Delaney
Peter Martin
John Kehoe
James Wall
Sylvester Doover
Peter Joyce
Anthony Gordon
Michael Ford
Daniel Ward

Edward Gildea
Joseph Zerinda
Andrew Slovinski
Thomas Gaffney
John Highstrick
Andrew Zmoiden
Patrick Ruane
Simon Mosock
Frank Shevskie
Anthony Teleskie
Peter Zavatskie
James Daly
John Hart
Michael Connell
Patrick Bolin
Dominick O'Malley
Thomas Barrett
Anthony Kane
John Gaffney
Owen Lee
Timothy Derrig

Thomas Wall
Michael Gaughan
Patrick Kelly
Martin Kilbride
Frank Kehoe
Robert Haston
M. J. Burke
James Burke

Thomas Duhig
John Cadarnis
Matt Teleski
Thomas Murphy
Joseph Costello
Anthony Coveloski
Anthony Nohenskie
Peter Bukoskie

STRIKING MINE WORKERS KILLED AT
LATTIMER MASSACRE
September 10, 1897

Broztowski, Sabastian
Cheslak, Michael
Chrzeszeski, _____
Czaja, Adalbert
Futa, John
Grekos, Anthony
Jurick, Steven
Kulick, _____
Jurechek, Andrew
Mieczkowski, Andrew

Monikaski, _____
Platek, Clement
Rekewicz, Rafael
Skrep, _____
Tarnowicz, John
Tomasantas, Jacob
Zagorski, _____
Ziominski, _____
Ziemba, _____

VICTIMS OF THE BALTIMORE TUNNEL EXPLOSION
June 5, 1919

Joseph Borden
John Brochoaski
Oscar Bidwell
William Bohn
Edmund Brew
Felix Boritz
Michael Burcha
John Burchta
George Bunza
Alick Cichon
Joseph Chesnock
Michael Cutlarski
Michael Connell
Fred Dippenworth
Stephen Demchack
Andrew Drevnock
Anthony Dzenis
Stanley Forestal

Nick Fedosh
Andrew Flecto
Bernard Gillespie
Gene Getner
Frank Gasner
John Golongo
Edward George
George Hanza
John Greglock
Joseph Hart
Michael Harris
Victor Harris
Andrew Hraber
Joseph Hopper
James Hern
William Hommick
William Hogan
John B. Jones

162

George Kubick
Walter Kubick
George Klepaer
John Kowatsko
Michael Kahwti
Andrew Kimcja
Paul Kuda
Harry Linteski
Joseph Lipenski
Patrick Lenahan
Michael Lestanes
Andrew Muroski
Lazlo Jiojavics
Joseph Mylefski
James Murphy
James Maguire
Charles Mantville
Paul Milchick
James J. McCloskey
John J. Michlosky
Anthony Narkunas
Michael Nestor
Edward Oliver
Patrick O'Malia
Charles Popherdinas
Michael Plachta
Llewellyn Perrett
Joseph Ponezin
John Penrish

John Pononish
Joseph Polinski
John Pochka
John Rushton
Michael Remakus
Joseph Repicka
Anthony Stanitis
John Stavenyash
Fred Spador
William Stenicka
Samuel Subiack
Stenley Smikel
Joseph Stremus
Alick Trucknick
Slaca Taminsky
Stanley Tavgonski
Stanley Terinski
Samuel Topeka
Adam Voychick
Kospy Vickesky
John J. Vannort
Michael Washick
Jacob Wozick
Frank Weichart
Richard Weichart
John Wallace
Joseph Yaris
John Yaskulski
John Zelinsky

KNOX DISASTER VICTIMS
January 22, 1959

Dominic Dovalesky
William Sinclair
Francis Bruno
Frank Orloski
John Bologa
David Stefanaitis

Herman Zalonis
Samuel Altieri
Benjamin Boyer
Joseph Gezenski
Eugene Ostroski
Charles Featherman

163

Bibliography

Books

Adamic, Louis; *Dynamite: The Story of Class Violence in America*, New York: Chelsea House Publishers, 1958. Reprint of 1936 publication.

American Catholic Thought on Social Questions, edited by Aaron I. Abett; Bobbs Merrill, 1968.

Aurand, Harold W.; *From the Molly Maguires to the United Mine Workers: The Social Ecology of an Industrial Union, 1869–1897*; Temple University Press, Philadelphia, Pa., 1971.

Berstein, Irving; *Turbulent Years, 1933–1941*; Houghton Mifflin, 1969.

Berthoff, Rowland Tappan, *British Immigrants in Industrial America*, Howard University Press, Cambridge, 1953.

Brookings Institute, *America's Capacity to Produce*, Washington, 1934.

Carver, Cecil; *John L. Lewis; Leader of Labor*, Robert Speller Publishing Corporation, New York, 1936.

Coleman, McAlister; *Men and Coal*, New York, Farrar, 1942.

Commonwealth of Pennsylvania, *Report of the Anthracite Coal Industry Commission*, Harrisburg, 1938.

Dubofsky, Melvyn and Van Tine, Warren; *John L. Lewis, A Biography*, Quadrangle, New York Times Book Co., New York, 1977.

Gallagher, Monsignor, John P.; *Scranton, Labor and Politics, 1870–1884*, Masters Thesis, Catholic University, Washington, 1965.

Gibbons, James Cardinal; *A Retrospect of Fifty Years*, John Murphy Co., 1916.

Glück, Elsie; *John Mitchell, Miner, Labor's Bargain with the Gilded Age*, The John Day Company, New York, 1929.

Jones, Eliot, *The Anthracite Coal Combination in the United States*; Cambridge, Harvard University Press, 1914.

Lens, Sidney; *The Labor Wars*, Doubleday and Company, Inc., Garden City, New York, 1973.

Merrick, Sister Mary Annunciata, R.S.M.; *A Case in Practical Democracy: Settlement of the Anthracite Coal Strike of 1902*, Dissertation, Ph.D., Notre Dame, September, 1942.

164

Mitchell, John; microfilm papers, King's College Library, Wilkes-Barre, Pa. from originals of Catholic University, Washington, D.C.

Nearing, Scott; *Anthracite*, Books for Libraries Press, Freeport, 1971.

Novak, Michael; *The Guns of Lattimer*, New York: Basic Books Incorporated Publishers, 1978.

Palmer, Henry W.; *Fifty Years at the Bar and in Politics*, Williamsport, Snyder and Bischof, 1913.

Powderly, Terence V.; *The Path I Trod*, edited by Harry J. Carman, Henry David and Paul Guthrie, Columbia University Press, New York, 1940.

Roberts, Ellis W., *Land Subsidence Caused by the Mining of Coal*, Ph.D., Dissertation, New York University, 1948.

Roberts, Peter; *Anthracite Coal Communities*, New York, MacMillan Company, 1904.

The Story of Anthracite, prepared and published by The Hudson Coal Company, New York, 1932.

The Autobiography of Mother Jones, edited by Mary Field Parton, Charles Kerr Publishing Company for Illinois Labor History Society, Chicago, 1980.

Walsh, Rev. Wiliam J.; *The United Mine Workers of America as an Economic and Social Force in the Anthracite Territory*, Ph.D. Dissertation, Catholic University, Washington, D.C., 1931. National Capital press, Inc., Washington, D.C. 1931.

Yellen, Samuel; *American Labor Struggle*, Harcourt Brace and Company, New York, 1936.

Legal and Legislative Sources

Luzerne Legal Register Reports; [Wilkes-Barre, Pa. Published by the Luzerne County Bar Association].

Purdons *Pennsylvania Statutes Annotated*, A compilation of Pennsylvania laws from 1700 to the present. Prepared by the publishers Editorial and West Publishing Company, St. Paul.

Thompson, J. W.; *Pennsylvania Mining Statutes Annotated*, Washington, D.C.: Government Printing Office, Department of Interior, Bureau of Mines.

Vale Pennsylvania Digest, Includes reports of Pennsylvania Superior and Supreme Courts. St. Paul; West Publishing Company.

Articles

Gendral, Fred; Luzerne and Its Miners. Sociology Term Paper, Harvard University. Available at Osterhout Free Library, Wilkes-Barre, Pa.

Kinneman, Marion Mack; "John Mitchell in Illinois," Illinois State University Journal.

Morris, James O.; "The Acquisitive Spirit of John Mitchell," U.M.W. President: Labor History.

Colliery Engineer and Metal Miner, Vol. 17, 1896. The Twin Shaft Disaster.

Newspapers

The Wilkes-Barre *Record*, January 1891 to June 1972.

The Wilkes-Barre *Record Almanac*, 1885 to 1961.

The Tri District News. Official organ of the United Mine Workers of America.

The Wilkes-Barre *Sunday Independent*, a weekly.

The Wilkes-Barre *Times-Leader Evening News*, January 1953 to June 1980.

The Citizens Voice, Wilkes-Barre daily 1978 to present.

The Wyoming *Observer*.

Scranton *Weekly Republican*; Saturday, September 11, 1869.

Photography Credits

Pennsylvania Historical Museum Commission, Anthracite Museum Complex.

The Lackawanna Historical Society, Mr. William Lewis, Director.

The Wyoming Historical and Geological Society, Mr. Bert Logan, Director.

Mike Burnside, Wyoming Historical and Geological Society.

The Hazleton Public Library, Mr. James Reinmiller, Director.

Holy Savior Church, Wilkes-Barre, The Rev. Joseph T. Conboy, Pastor.

Stephen Lukasik, Photographer, Dupont, Pa.

Bernard Walko, Photographer, Edwardsville, Pa.

Ivor Williams, Nanticoke.

United States Department of Interior, Bureau of Mines.

166